Timothy Mo

MANCHESTER
UNIVERSITY PRESS

CONTEMPORARY WORLD WRITERS

SERIES EDITOR   JOHN THIEME

ALREADY PUBLISHED IN THE SERIES

Peter Carey   BRUCE WOODCOCK
Toni Morrison   JILL MATUS
Alice Munro   CORAL ANN HOWELLS
Ngugi Wa Thiong'o   PATRICK WILLIAMS
Salman Rushdie   CATHERINE CUNDY
Derek Walcott   JOHN THIEME

FORTHCOMING

Anita Desai   SHIRLEY CHEW
Kazuo Ishiguro   BARRY LEWIS
Hanif Kureishi   BART MOORE-GILBERT
Les Murray   STEVEN MATTHEWS
Caryl Phillips   BENEDICTE LEDENT
Wole Soyinka   ABDULRAZAK GURNAH

Timothy Mo

ELAINE YEE LIN HO

Manchester University Press

Manchester and New York

distributed exclusively in the USA by St. Martin's Press

The right of Elaine Yee Lin Ho to be identified as the author of this work has been asserted by her in accordance with the Copyright, Designs and Patents Act 1988.

Published by Manchester University Press
Oxford Road, Manchester M13 9NR, UK
and Room 400, 175 Fifth Avenue, New York, NY 10010, USA
http://www.manchesteruniversitypress.co.uk

Distributed exclusively in the USA by
St. Martin's Press, Inc., 175 Fifth Avenue, New York, NY 10010, USA

Distributed exclusively in Canada by
UBC Press, University of British Columbia, 2029 West Mall,
Vancouver, BC, Canada V6T 1Z2

British Library Cataloguing-in-Publication Data
A catalogue record for this book is available from the British Library

Library of Congress Cataloging-in-Publication Data applied for

ISBN 0 7190 5389 7 *hardback*
    0 7190 5390 0 *paperback*

First published 2000
06 05 04 03 02 01 00   10 9 8 7 6 5 4 3 2 1

Typeset in Aldus
by Koinonia, Manchester
Printed in Great Britain
by Bell and Bain Ltd, Glasgow

To the memory of my mother

Contents

ACKNOWLEDGEMENTS viii
SERIES EDITOR'S FOREWORD ix
CHRONOLOGY xi

1 Contexts and intertexts 1

2 The Chinese family at home: *The Monkey King* 29

3 The Chinese family in diaspora: *Sour Sweet* 50

4 History from the margins: *An Insular Possession* 69

5 The nation and its others: *The Redundancy of Courage* 88

6 Home and the world: *Brownout on Breadfruit Boulevard* 109

7 *Renegade or Halo²*: a postscript 127

8 Critical overview and conclusion 144

NOTES 149
SELECT BIBLIOGRAPHY 169
INDEX 179

Acknowledgements

I am grateful to the Research Grants Council, Hong Kong, for a research grant in support of the writing of this book, and to my research assistant, Gaye Gould, for her patience, efficiency, and work beyond the call of duty. In Hong Kong, I would like to thank Christopher Hutton, Douglas Kerr, Shirley Lim, Estella Tong, Q. S. Tong; in Britain, Shirley Chew, Alan Durant, Andrew Gibson, Tom Healy, Robert Young. To John Thieme, General Editor of the *Contemporary World Writers* Series, I owe a debt of gratitude for the opportunity to write this book; he has been unfailing in his support, and I could not have had better editorial advice. The courtesy and goodwill of Matthew Frost at Manchester University Press gave the enjoyable process of writing this book an additional pleasure.

ELAINE YEE LIN HO
University of Hong Kong

Series editor's foreword

Contemporary World Writers is an innovative series of authoritative introductions to a range of culturally diverse contemporary writers from outside Britain and the United States, or from 'minority' backgrounds within Britain or the United States. In addition to providing comprehensive general introductions, books in the series also argue stimulating original theses, often but not always related to contemporary debates in post-colonial studies.

The series locates individual writers within their specific cultural contexts, while recognising that such contexts are themselves invariably a complex mixture of hybridised influences. It aims to counter tendencies to appropriate the writers discussed into the canon of English or American literature or to regard them as 'other'.

Each volume includes a chronology of the writer's life, an introductory section on formative contexts and intertexts, discussion of all the writer's major works, a bibliography of primary and secondary works and an index. Issues of racial, national and cultural identity are explored, as are gender and sexuality. Books in the series also examine writers' use of genre, particularly ways in which Western genres are adapted or subverted and 'traditional' local forms are reworked in a contemporary context.

Contemporary World Writers aims to bring together the theoretical impulse which currently dominates post-colonial studies and closely argued readings of particular authors' works, and by so doing to avoid the danger of appropriating the specifics of particular texts into the hegemony of totalising theories.

Chronology

1950   Born 30 December in Hong Kong. Father Hong Kong Chinese lawyer; mother, Yorkshire–Welsh, working class; parents divorced when he was 18 months old. Educated in the Convent of the Precious Blood.

1960   Leaves Hong Kong, attends Prep School in Finchley, north London, and then Mill Hill School, north London.

1969   Enters St John's College, Oxford, reads History.

1971   Wins Gibbs Prize.

1972   Graduates from Oxford. Begins writing *The Monkey King*

1975–6 Works at the *Times Educational Supplement* for eighteen months, and then as part-time editor at *New Statesman*; works as part-time PAYE clerk, and as a trainer in a gym.

1976   Works as part-time reporter for *Boxing News*, paid an advance of £500 for *The Monkey King*.

1978   *The Monkey King* published by André Deutsch.

1979   *The Monkey King* wins the Geoffrey Faber Memorial Prize. Receives £1000 advance from André Deutsch for *Sour Sweet*.

1982   *Sour Sweet* published; short-listed for the Booker Prize and the Whitbread Prize.

1983   *Sour Sweet* wins the Hawthornden Prize.

1986   *An Insular Possession* published by Chatto & Windus; short listed for the Booker Prize.

1990   Quits reporting for *Boxing News*.

1991   *The Redundancy of Courage* published by Chatto & Windus; short-listed for the Booker Prize.

1992   Receives E. M. Forster Award from the American Academy of Arts and Letters.

1993   Rejects advance for next novel by Chatto and Windus.

1995   Sets up his own private press, Paddleless Press. *Brownout on Breadfruit Boulevard* published by Paddleless Press.

1999   *Renegade or Halo*^{2} published by Paddleless Press.

Contexts and intertexts

BORN in 1950 of a Cantonese-Chinese father and Welsh–
Yorkshire mother, Timothy Mo spent his first nine years in
Hong Kong where he attended first the Convent of the Precious
Blood, a local Chinese-medium school run by Cantonese nuns,
and then Quarry Bay international school, where the medium of
instruction is English. At the age of ten, he left for England and,
after completing his secondary education at Mill Hill School,
went on to read History at Oxford. On graduation, Mo worked
for various publications, including the *Times Educational Supplement* and the *New Statesman*, before starting a more permanent
job as a writer for *Boxing News*. His literary career began to take
shape with the publication, in 1978, of his first novel, *The
Monkey King*, which won the Geoffrey Faber Memorial Prize.
His second novel, *Sour Sweet*, appeared in 1982, and was awarded
the Hawthornden Prize; it was later adapted into a film although
Mo played little part in either the script or the shooting.
Another four-year hiatus separated *Sour Sweet* from his third
novel, *An Insular Possession* (1986), which was followed in 1991
by *The Redundancy of Courage*. *An Insular Possession* was
short-listed for the Booker Prize, and in 1992, Mo received the
E. M. Forster Award from the American Academy of Arts and
Letters. His two most recent novels, *Brownout on Breadfruit
Boulevard* (1995) and *Renegade or Halo*[2] (1999), were published
by Paddleless Press which he set up himself.[1]

The publication of *The Monkey King* and especially *Sour
Sweet* in the late 1970s and early 1980s stands as one of the

significant landmarks in contemporary British literature. The arrival in London of writers from former British colonial outposts had generated a current of change which was gathering momentum. The work of Sam Selvon and V. S. Naipaul, followed by that of Salman Rushdie, speak not only of distant shores and locations, but clearly signal their presence in British society. Before Mo, these writers were prominent among those who were creating an alternative fiction fuelled by the dynamics of their own trans-national and cross-cultural provenance. Mo's early novels added an ethnic Chinese contour to the new literary map of British fiction, and with Kazuo Ishiguro's *A Pale View of Hills* (1982), which appeared in the same year as *Sour Sweet*, British readers were also made aware of the previously invisible Japanese minority on their shores.

The writers of Mo's generation who emerged in the 1970s and early 1980s bear witness to the changing cultural form-ations of the post-colonial world in which not only the former colonies but also Britain itself, as a post-imperial power, has to find its place. For many of Mo's predecessors and contempor-aries, their personal and ancestral histories begin in ethnic cultures outside Britain, and their creative inspiration and, often, cultural affiliations are formed out of this early experi-ence. Such experience is complicated by exposure, often through education, to British institutions and discourses of learning, and individual writers show the different ways in which such complication shapes their creativity. As colonials themselves or the subjects of former colonies, their perceptions of Britain from afar, and the differences between such perceptions and the actual experience of British society onshore, are a rich source of narrative. Migration to Britain and subsequent settlement also enable critical vantages on their ethnic cultures of origin and present affiliations to their ethnic communities in Britain. The hardship of living and being treated as aliens in Britain, and the attenuation of ethnic bonds, are themes frequently rehearsed. However, these tragic themes of unbelonging and deculturation co-exist with celebrations of subjects liberated from the frames of single cultures and capable of holding in themselves multiple and conflictual vantages on British or any individual ethnic culture. Crossing the inherited boundaries within cultures, they often challenge the unitary drives of the nation-state, and the agendas of class, ethnic and gender hegemony. In transforming the literary geography of contemporary British literature, the fiction of Mo and those writers of his generation helps to institute post-imperial Britain's emergence as a multi-ethnic and multicultural nation. Crossing between nations, these writers and their fictional characters can be seen as enacting identities which transgress the rigid and artificial boundaries of the nation-state. Thus, there is both a British and a global dimension to the making of these authors and their work, and the inter-cultural and inter-national significance of their fiction can be seen on both the British and world literary stages.

In academic discourses, if English literature used to be traditionally defined by writing from the British Isles, this new fiction has a doubled belonging – to British literature, and to literatures in English written and published from locations round the world. Once again, the provenance of the writers as well as the subject matter of their narratives destabilise conventional categories, both in academic discourses and popular recognition.[2] My discussion of Mo in this book is very much framed by postcolonial theories of literary and cultural production although this is a critical rather than a theoretical study. One of the themes – which I see as a problematic, a structure of questions and answers – I wish to introduce and pursue throughout is that of identity, specifically the formations of identities and the contest, within specific cultural milieus, of majority and marginal identities. Mo's novels have strong protagonist figures, and they will provide the foci of my discussions of individual works in the chapters of this book. By devoting one chapter each to the six novels, it will be possible to look in detail at the novels as different experimentations with narrative, and the generic forms and conventions which Mo rehearses and transforms. At the same time, the cross-referencing of common themes and problematics will show how changes in narrative embody Mo's many returns, through multiple routings, to those urgent preoccupations about identity and, in particular, to contextualise these preoccupations in communities and cultures that are either neglected or unfamiliar.

In discussing the late twentieth-century connection between the multivocality of Literature in English and questions of identity, Bruce King observed: 'The new national literatures, national multicultural literatures and International English literature were parts of a developing urban global culture, produced by international politics, communications and a world-wide economy, which include a heightened awareness of difference partly to assert identity.'[3] 'A heightened awareness of difference partly to assert identity': King's observation postulates the two key terms, 'difference' and 'identity', which often co-exist uneasily in contemporary narratives of societies and cultures. Mo's novels are preoccupied with the relationship between these two terms, and these preoccupations help to situate them as significant landmarks on a globalised literary and academic domain. The relationship between the two terms can be explored from a number of vantages which Mo's fiction – like those of his contemporaries – both represents and problematises. From one of these vantages, as Stuart Hall notes, cultural identity can be seen in terms of 'one, shared culture, a sort of collective "one true self" … which people with a shared history and ancestry hold in common… This "oneness", underlying all the other, more superficial differences' (223)[4] is the key to some of Mo's characters' self-understanding and location within a particular collective or community. Often, it is the experience of change, or difference, which makes integration and unity an imperative; indeed, the more extreme the difference – as a condition of displacement or subjugation – the more urgent the project of constructing or imagining 'oneness' becomes. In Mo's novels, identity as 'oneness' is often explored in the context of radical changes he imagines and narrates, in particular those generated by migration, exile, and marginality which, in turn, produce that 'heightened awareness' that Bruce King referred to.

A second vantage, to quote again from Stuart Hall, recognises that 'as well as the many points of similarity, there are also critical points of deep and significant *difference* which constitute "what we really are"; or rather – since history has intervened – "what we have become". We cannot speak for very long, with any exactness, about "one experience, one identity", without acknowledging its other side – the ruptures and discontinuities which constitute, precisely, "uniqueness"'(225, italics in original). For many of Mo's characters – each in their own way – the impact of difference externally imposed or its emergence into subjective consciousness is also the moment of crisis. Because of Mo's interest in character as narrative, the crisis for individuals takes on much broader historical, social and cultural significance. It can be read allegorically, as referring to a larger crisis of community, or symptomatically, in pointing towards those hidden transformations and traumas through which cultures change and renew themselves in time.

These complex negotiations of identity, difference and narrative begin, for Mo, within a specifically Chinese milieu. But while Mo's Chinese ancestry might very well have shaped these beginnings, the issues that he raises and explores are by no means exclusive to the Chinese milieu. Before moving on to a detailed discussion of some of these issues, it is worth noting that Mo's choice of fictional location and subject matter are topical, and even prescient, in the sense that his imaginative access to certain communities and cultures antedates and anticipates popular attention to them. *The Monkey King* and *Sour Sweet*, as I have noted earlier on, precede the explosions of interest of British literature and the reading public in ethnic communities and subjects. *An Insular Possession*, which narrates events leading to Hong Kong's colonisation in the nineteenth century, appeared in 1986, only two years after the signing of the Joint Declaration which determined Hong Kong's return to China, at a time of equable relations between Britain and China when the struggles of the past seemed forever interred. In the light of the developing conflict between Britain and China during the years leading up to 1997, Mo's reinvention of the past in *An Insular Possession* also takes on the quality of a kind of prediction. In *The Redundancy of Courage*, the fictional location of Danu has significant parallels with East Timor, again drawing readers to a remote site of colonial and postcolonial conflict before it was to capture world attention. In the wake of the people's revolution which overthrew the Marcos government, *Brownout on Breadfruit Boulevard*, set in the Philippines, was certainly topical, and it remains to be seen if Mo's robust fictional analysis of that country's tortuous situation will develop a predictive capacity. *Renegade or Halo²*, Mo's latest novel to date, turns its attention to another invisible community, the illegal migrant workers whose journeys across the globe are rarely the subject of contemporary fiction in English.

Because of their plural ethno-cultural allegiances, Mo's protagonists often find themselves on the margins of structures in the grip of a dominant and inherited tradition. Set in Hong Kong in the 1950s and 1960s, *The Monkey King* chronicles the fortunes of a Cantonese family, the Poons. Written as a third-person narrative, the novel focuses on the observations and experience of Wallace Nolasco, the Macau-born son-in-law, and his struggles with the patriarch, Mr Poon. *Sour Sweet* continues to explore the Chinese family from the inside, but shifts its location to London in the 1960s. The woman protagonist, Lily Chen, lives within the enclosed, semi-autonomous enclave of her family, having, and preferring to have, little contact with suburban British society. Already in these two novels, we see Mo's interest in characters who, for reasons of birth and history, by choice or accident, are peripheral to the social milieu they inhabit. This interest continues and develops an alternative focus and scope in *An Insular Possession*, which transforms into fictional pageant the historical conflict between China and Britain in the early nineteenth century which led to the first Opium War and the colonisation of Hong Kong in 1842. With its congeries of fact and fiction, plural generic forms and styles, and narrative focalisation through two American protagonists, *An Insular Possession* problematises the realist mode which Mo had used to great effect in *The Monkey King* and *Sour Sweet*, and tells a story of two empires from the point of view of peripheral characters who have no vested interest in the success or decline and fall of either of them. A kind of non-partisan narrative begins to emerge in *An Insular Possession* which is again rehearsed in Mo's fourth novel, *The Redundancy of Courage*, the first one to have a first-person narrator, Adolph Ng. Ng is of Chinese ancestry but what interests Mo is his situation as a reluctant participant in Danu's struggle against colonialism; Ng's loyalty to the Danuese cause is as mobile as his shifting eye on events. In many ways, *The Redundancy of Courage* pushes to the edge Mo's fictional investment in marginals and their stories by calling into question the ethics, and hence the authority, of its non-aligned narrator. *Brownout on Breadfruit Boulevard* is riddled with scepticism about those who self-consciously stake their claim as marginals in the contemporary global conflict of cultures. The novel mimics their self-righteous rhetoric, and pierces what it sees as their facade of radicalism, behind which the ancient corruptions of power and greed circulate with unabated energy. The true marginals are elsewhere, to be found in the migrant society which *Renegade or Halo*[2] brings into view.

In pursuing and doubling back on the themes of marginal identities and histories, Mo displays considerable stylistic panache and imaginative daring. His novels are mostly written as realist fictions sharpened by the knife of satire. And the knife twists and turns, probing, dissecting, anatomising. Traditionally, satire, as Claude Rawson reminds us, is 'an instrument of aggression'.[5] As a satirist, Mo is a risk-taker; nothing seems to be sacred to him. Chinese culture is demystified with little ceremony. And as he delves into the issues of oppression, resistance and victimhood in other places and cultures, Mo refuses to take sides, and indeed goes out of his way sometimes to ensure that none of his fictional subjects and the positions they embody remain unscathed. But in the fault lines of the powerful structures he satirises, Mo also finds a lot that engages his sympathy, and his pugnacious wit is frequently relieved by bursts of good-humoured laughter. As an author, Mo likes his characters; in their foibles and folly, he sees the absurdity innate in the human desire to order the ineluctable chaos of their lives. The author-as-satirist revels in the vanity of human wishes, and feeds on it with consummate delight, although, in the later novels, where the best-laid plans for self and society always go awry, Mo's comic satire delivers a much more cynical punch. His prose and choice of satiric targets speak to a highly cultivated taste for the arts of hand-to-hand combat. A favourite reference point for both Mo and his interviewers is his work as a reporter for *Boxing News*, and its stark contrast with the solitary enterprise of fiction-writing. But in his rhetoric, Mo blurs the boundaries between the physical and the contemplative life; needling, teasing, inviting, repelling, Mo recreates in language the strategies and rhythms of boxing, his favourite spectator sport.

In a recent essay, with the intriguing title 'Fighting their Writing', Mo reminisces about his childhood tutelage in Hong Kong under the pugilistic Mr Tingle. He writes, 'right from the start flurries of fists held no terrors for me. I had an affinity for the gloves, dank with the clammy hands of previous users and prickly with horse-hair as they were' (301).[6] Under Mr Tingle, whom Mo fondly remembers, this natural affinity was quickly developed so that at the age of eight, Mo won his first boxing match – the only one of his team to do so. The victory, however, would not have been possible without the strict discipline – old-fashioned but effective – which Mr Tingle's training regime enforced, and which Mo the writer speaks of eloquently in the following terms: 'There is a grammar of combat, a syntax of movement, which the human body has to obey in all fighting systems, just as there are less iron rules governing language and communication' (304). From the disciplining of the body, Mo's metaphorical mapping of fighting and writing extends to the strategies of combat or what he calls 'the unbreakable grammatical principles' (310) of the fight which he recounts in detail, although, with customary bravado, he goes on to state that 'some of these rules are less than prescriptive for those with the talent to flout them (just as great novelists can ignore the elementary rules of the novel)' (311).

In the stylish transference of metaphors between the discourses of fighting and language, and deliberate analogies and oppositions between his writing and reading and martial arts, Mo fashions a complex self-identity. To remember his childhood – and here it makes not the slightest difference how accurate or inaccurate that memory may be – is to explore the parameters of his identity formation. We are offered a narrative which foregrounds his engagement with both the active and the contemplative life. In the light of memory, Mo appears as the subject of multiple discourses, yoking in himself the literary and the martial, not only unfazed but positively energised by their contradiction. This memory is the ground of his transgressive creativity which, in turn, shapes the distinctive pugnacity of his fictional language.

There is an important cultural sub-text to this. In the essay, Mo frequently draws together and juxtaposes the British and Chinese influences on his early life, which are as important to his cultural identity as they are to his understanding of the differences between the martial arts of east and west. Though professing abhorrence for the word 'culture' – 'when I see the word "culture" ', he says, 'I reach for my *eskrima* staves' (299) – the essay is steeped in cultural references, from the names of famous British authors he has read since childhood to the 'specialist' appraisal of western boxing and various 'oriental weapon systems' (315). Even more significantly, Mo presents himself as someone who can, and is not afraid to, judge the relative merits of his cultural influences. The accident of birth has given him access to two radically different cultures, but a cultural relativist he is not. Mr Tingle was an Australian but he was 'naturally, more English than the English' (300) and his pupil, though not yet consciously an Anglophile in the early days, clearly found his boxing master much more congenial than his Chinese teachers. Mo's failure at calligraphy class bred in him an early dislike of Chinese classical education which was intensified by the 'ferocious' Cantonese nuns who were his teachers at the Convent of the Precious Blood (305). With the benefit of mature reflection, he thinks of himself as 'endowed through genes and upbringing with a precocious conceptual intelligence, adrift within an ideographic literary culture' (305), and there is no question in his mind that the Chinese pedagogic system and the world view it encodes would have failed him even worse had he not made an early escape into the British fold. In contrast to his relish for the robust adversarial individualism embodied by Mr Tingle, Mo admits that he has never adjusted to what he calls 'the maddening circular logic of traditional Chinese dialectic', especially what he sees as the Chinese preferences for 'a middle position between opinions' (307). It is an unusually revealing insight, tucked away in this anecdote of childhood.[7] Mo's choice, as the essay is keen to demonstrate, is made very early on, unselfconsciously and unintentionally, and it permeates his adult convictions and writing, and his preferences both literary and cultural.[8]

The breathtaking transitions between the languages of fighting and literature enact the two dynamic forces of the title – fighting and writing – that have shaped Mo's identity. Mo endorses boxing and fencing in the same breath as he rehearses his favourite British authors; at the same time, his dismissal of oriental weapon systems as 'philosophically … flatulent' (315) is accompanied by the cheeky comment that the ancient Book of Five Rings by a Japanese duellist is 'a Nipponese disinformation exercise' (315). When he talks about his reading, in this essay or elsewhere, Mo does not mention a single Chinese writer, and while he acknowledges sources on Chinese subject matter he consulted in the writing of his novels, these tend to be written by English authors. The late sixteenth-century Chinese classic, *The Journey to the West*, which has inspired the title and characterisation of Wallace in *The Monkey King*, is well-known enough in folk tale and oral versions. In an interview for a Taiwanese literary journal, Mo claims to have read the original novel but specifies that it is the image of the Monkey that he has been most familiar with ever since reading comic-strip adaptations as a child;[9] there is little evidence to suggest that he is interested in the elaborate Buddhist arguments of the novel. Fighting, like writing, encodes and enacts the self-identity and world view of a culture. Through his experience with both art-forms, Mo judges and discriminates the eastern and western cultures he crosses in a hierarchy of merit.

A cultivated interest in the arts of combat grows and deepens through knowledge of the martial arts systems from different cultures, and cultural comparison encourages a kind of cultural relativism. But when Mo actually fights – or judges – there is no middle ground of relative merit, only a winner and a loser. Mo is keenly aware of these contradictions in his engagements with culture through fighting and writing, and much more personally, as a hybrid impelled by the will to choose between his cultures of affiliation. He acts like a fighter who must win or lose. The cornerstone of his commitment as a writer is the ability and the courage to profess and demonstrate his cultural allegiances and choices, even if it means going against the grain of received opinion or common prejudices. 'To write in plain, vigorous language,' said George Orwell, 'one has to think fearlessly, and if one thinks fearlessly one cannot be politically orthodox.'[10] While appreciating Mo's courage, we must remember that one of satire's traditional aims, 'the hurtful and the punitive',[11] quite often provides its primary motivation. Beginning with his attacks on Chinese culture, Mo has also shown strategic calculation, over the past two decades, in the choice of satiric targets. They court controversy for reasons one can only speculate on: to rehearse private convictions in fiction and public debate, to sell books or even simply an irrepressible urge to offend. A future biographer might take up the task of disentangling the motives, pure or impure, behind Mo's satiric creativity. Here, what I wish to plot are some of the intersections between Mo's fictional thematics and his engagements, in the public sphere, with arguments about cultural identity.

A 'Chinese' writer

Because of Mo's hybrid provenance, his British nationality and residence – at least until recently – and the subject matter of his novels, it is possible to situate his work in different literary and cultural contexts. But at the start of his career in the late 1970s and early 1980s, the public image of Mo, as it emerged in reviews of his books in the British literary press, focuses on his Chinese ancestry and early life in a Chinese family in Hong Kong. This, in turn, is supposed to have given him a privileged insider view of Chinese culture. Given the subject matter of both *The Monkey King* and *Sour Sweet*, and the Chinese ethnicity of the major characters, this reception is hardly surprising. It is also worth noting that Mo's novels were very much welcomed precisely because they were the first to give a voice, an identity, and a central literary place to an ethnic community of which the British reading public had little knowledge and understanding. For example, Peter Lewis reflected as follows on *Sour Sweet*: 'As in *The Monkey King*, Mo provides us with an inside view of an unfamiliar social milieu, but by placing the narrative firmly in London, he achieves a new *frisson*. What is startling is the apparent discrepancy between location and action, between modern England and a largely self-contained and alien world functioning within it.'[12] And William Boyd observed facetiously that after reading *Sour Sweet*, no one could enter a Chinese restaurant in Britain again without feeling like 'a total idiot'.[13]

But right from the start, Mo has vigorously contested the public reception of him as a Chinese writer, or an insider to Chinese culture. He has always insisted that his ethnicity is not the issue, and in public pronouncements, has frequently disclaimed any privileged knowledge of Chinese culture and community. Noting the responses to his narrative of Chinatown in *Sour Sweet*, Mo professes himself bemused: 'It's a little bit strange being a great authority on what goes on in Chinese restaurants. I'm probably as ignorant as anyone else.'[14] To Ishiguro, he admits that he is '[a] complete outsider' to Chinatown.[15] The theme of *Sour Sweet*, he states in another interview, 'was the unity of good and bad... It wasn't about Chinese people living in London. That was really incidental... They're not people I've ever met or known. I don't know anyone from Chinatown.'[16] And taking his denial even further, Mo declares, 'I know nothing about Chinese culture. It is as hard for me to write about things Chinese as it must have been for Paul Scott or J. G. Farrell to write about India. I'm a Brit.'[17]

The disclaimer of special interest in the 'Chinese' is entirely consistent with Mo's wholesale disparagement of his own early experience of the culture in Hong Kong. However, it is useful to remember that in the convention of satire, satirists often dissociate themselves personally from their targets. Here again, Claude Rawson's insights on the satiric tradition may offer us a particular, formal vantage on what Mo has done. Rawson observes, 'It was precisely because the essential purpose was aggressive that the [satiric] poet needed to convince himself and others that he was not personally vindictive or anti-social. Apologies for satire quickly became commonplace in satire.'[18] Mo's conscious positioning away from 'Chineseness', both his own and others', can be seen as a satirist's defence, even though it falls short of the conventional apology.

This formal caveat aside, Mo's quarrel with the reviewers over the 'Chinese' labelling is highly significant in two contexts: first, in the complicated treatment of the thematics of identity in his novels, and second, in the politics of identity in contemporary British literature. Leaving aside for the moment the issue of Mo's self-professed 'Britishness', his novels actually problematise and disable the kind of summary conclusions about 'Chineseness' that the reviewers' labelling of him implies. In Wallace Nolasco of *The Monkey King* and Lily Chen of *Sour Sweet*, Mo addresses the question of what are the most critical perspectives from which Chinese culture can be observed. Contrary to certain arguments which champion the privileged vantage of the insider,[19] Mo creates two subjects who are both inside and outside the Chinese family and by implication, inside and outside Chinese culture. Through them, Mo delivers some of his sharpest criticism of the culture in terms entirely consistent with his observations in 'Fighting their Writing'. A further and more fundamental critique that these characters institute is of the concept and misguided claims of the cultural insider. Mo offers significant insights on cultural identity as a flexible construct in which inherited tradition, self-perception and external imposition are in constant negotiation; a construct which is subject to the contrary pulls of the conscious and the unconscious and is never fixed or fixable. Through these protagonists and their stories, Mo anticipates, or concretises, some of the abstract issues that are debated in the different approaches – ethnographical, psychoanalytical, temporal–spatial – to cultural identity now current in academic discourses.[20] In this light, it is not difficult to see why he so vigorously contests the reviewers' assignment of him as a 'Chinese' writer and insider; it is reductive, not only of his own aims and achievements as a writer, but also of the project of understanding cultural identity itself. It is as convenient, and misleading, as the pigeon-holing of Naipaul as a Caribbean or Rushdie as an Indian writer.

Wallace Nolasco is a Macanese of Portuguese descent; though married into a Cantonese family, he remains for a long time an outsider both in terms of his own self-identification and his ostracisation by the other family members. But having lived among Chinese people for a long time, and now as one of their kind, Wallace is familiar with their ways of life, rituals and idiosyncrasies. Mo clearly relishes the advantages but also the contradictions inherent in Wallace's situation. It is part of the novel's argument that location and social experience determine the way we look at ourselves and the world, and Wallace's perspective is necessarily doubled, a hybrid of his situation as both outsider and insider.

Unlike Wallace, Lily sees herself as completely and purely Chinese; her ethnicity is immune to change in time and place and can never be diluted. But that is only part of her story in *Sour Sweet*. As an immigrant in London who has little contact with other Chinese people either in her natal place or adopted country, Lily is an ethnic exile, cut off from the community to which she feels and professes an inalienable sense of belonging. Her only location is her immediate family, and her 'Chineseness', as we shall see in detail in Chapter Three, speaks of an imaginary cultural tradition and bond which she remembers from time to time to justify habitual practices in family life. An

invented tradition, memory and practice: these are the constituents of Lily's 'Chineseness'. Though she considers all other
Chinese people to be like herself, and will not admit otherwise,
the novel shows very clearly that even with the members of her
own family, what it means to be 'Chinese' is the subject of
difference. In some ways, the reviewers were correct: Mo's
characters do think of themselves as insiders to Chinese culture
and Mo himself is both knowledgeable and knowing. But the
problematic location of Wallace and Lily in the novels clearly
indicates that their claims to insider knowledge have a hint of
desperation, and are a function of their eccentricity, their
distance from the centre, their exile. Furthermore, the representations of 'Chineseness' in the novels are as varied as the
characters themselves, exemplifying both sameness and difference. Who then is 'Chinese'? Who is an insider?

With *An Insular Possession*, Mo turns his back on Chinese
characters and culture. In interviews, he has described the first
two novels as 'exercises', in the manner of literary predecessors
who dismiss their early work as so much necessary training or
juvenilia. *An Insular Possession* takes place in a Chinese setting,
but none of its significant characters is Chinese; and by choosing
an earlier historical moment, Mo makes the point that he, like
any other writer with historical imagination, is an outsider
trying to find his way into the past, that foreign country. In the
traditional rites of this passage, texts are the medium and scholarship is the key, but the novel is sceptical that the performance of
these rites can guarantee a writer's arrival at some destination of
historical truth. The writer may develop a more knowledgeable
understanding of the period he narrates, and an ability to see its
subjects empathetically. But he cannot become an insider, not
simply because of the irrecoverable distance in time but, more
importantly, because the grounds on which traditional claims
are made to insider knowledge – what it was really like – have
been completely destabilised by contemporary scepticism. His
two American protagonists, the journalists Gideon Chase and
Walter Eastman, align themselves with the Chinese against the
British, and report on Chinese customs and the Chinese

experience of British imperial aggression. Like his protagonists, Mo the historical novelist attempts to cross boundaries, to make the unknown known. Both the author and his characters are really attempting the impossible, but Mo undertakes his narrative with a clear historicist's awareness of this fatal condition.[21]

Although Adolph Ng in *The Redundancy of Courage* is of Chinese ancestry and the novel briefly refers to the diasporal Chinese community in Danu, the significant point about Ng is that he has or professes no ethnic affiliations. Chinese, natives, *mestizos, malais*: in successive moments of political and military conflict, he is incorporated into each of these ethnic groups that make up the Danuese nation. But his querulous first-person voice registers his discontent with an identity imposed by the accidents of belonging, or circumscribed by the power which any group can exercise over others at different times. Ng the marginal is unheroic; but the battle for ethnic and national determinations of individual identity is itself a dubious cause of heroism. In *The Redundancy of Courage*, identity is a struggle in which there are only losers. But if the project of identity always requires a victim – as *Redundancy* suggests – Mo, in *Brownout on Breadfruit Boulevard*, also shows how the claims of victimhood are, in turn, structured by the dubious ethics of competition which mirror the struggles for political power. *Brownout* assembles a cast of characters who claim to be victims; in this novel, victims victimise each other, and in the process, transform into victims characters living otherwise unperplexed lives. And most recently, in *Renegade or Halo²*, Mo shows how in a global underclass, a national identity is dispersed and reconstituted through diasporal contact and confrontation with a host of others.

Mo's resistance against being labelled a 'Chinese' writer is consistent with his fictions of identity. Beginning with a fight against an imposed identity early on in his career, Mo, in *Renegade or Halo²*, extends and pushes to the edge his field of combat. We can see in Mo's struggle with reviewers an early performance of identity as a cultural process in which biological and ethnic origins, external assignment and self-decision are in uneven and unstable interaction. The performance and the process are ongoing; as Mo moves away from a Chinese milieu and Chinese subjects in his later novels, his own ethnic identity recedes as an issue. But the process of his identity is by no means resolved or concluded, and as we have seen, his novels continue to explore projects of identity in different times and places.

'I'm a Brit'

The stark opposition – Chinese or British – which Mo as an adult writer constructs and feels compelled to choose between is belied by the racially and culturally heterogeneous environment of his early days in Hong Kong which he remembers in 'Fighting their Writing', and especially in 'One of Billy's Boys'. The vivid personalities surfacing in the cauldron of childhood exemplify this heterogeneity; chief among them is Mo himself, Eurasian, and brought up by Chinese amahs in the British household of his stepfather. They include also a young woman teacher from New Zealand; Mr Tingle, an Anglophile Australian; Tingle's boys, Chinese and British, in their red and blue corners; and the nuns of the Precious Blood convent. The 'Hong Kong' which Mo remembers in the two articles is the space where different races and cultures cohabit but also form their own enclaves, and Mo, in his memory, both brings them together and observes their boundaries. This mutually exclusive cohabitation which is 'Hong Kong' appears also in *The Monkey King*. Mo, in his self-fashioning, is the paradoxical subject who crosses and yet insists on boundaries. I will return to the mimesis of 'Hong Kong' in Mo's fiction in the chapters on *The Monkey King* and *An Insular Possession*.

What are we to make of Mo's cryptic declaration, 'I'm a Brit'? In its immediate context, it is obviously a challenge to the reviewers, and reinstates that aspect of his culture and identity which their emphasis on his 'Chineseness' has thrown out of focus. In declaring publicly his choice, Mo asserts the individual's right to choose his identity and cultural affiliation against a powerful discursive establishment which has, consciously or inadvertently, assigned him a place. When the reviewers first described him and his novels as 'Chinese', it could be seen as a demarcation of their separateness: an author from an ethnic minority whose cultural productions are marginal, unfamiliar, or even alien, to the British mainstream. It was also probably in part an attempt to include him in what was coming to look like a movement, another designated stripe in the rainbow of the new multi-ethnic British novel. It is characteristic, but not necessarily a misprision, that Mo saw this as an act of exclusion, and responded with the strident self-declaration as 'a Brit'. This is one way of looking at the issue in which Mo's declaration appears as a radical gesture of autonomy. But it is also a gesture that is becoming outdated as a newer and more recent generation of British writers speak with confidence of their ethnic affiliations. Mo's career to date has spanned the decades when the ethnic and cultural map of Britain has undergone rapid change. In the unfolding complications of what it means to be 'British' over the past decade, the reductive opposition between 'British' and 'Chinese' seen in Mo's earlier struggle could hardly be sustained. At the same time, this opposition cannot really contain the complex issues in our changing understanding of the project of identity.

Beneath Mo's various statements about being 'British' or 'Chinese' are certain assumptions about ethnicity and culture that are in themselves problematic. Again, the reviewers may not be at fault; what they did was to gloss one aspect of Mo's dual heritage, and to justify this, they could rightly point to the subject matter of his first two novels. Mo's dispute with this labelling is entirely consistent with his disparagement of Chinese culture, and his professed dislike of what he sees as its orthodox character. It is, of course, not a problem for authors to be critical of their own cultures. The issue here is rather that Mo has taken a structural view of Chinese culture which, first, reduces it to a number of discernible and largely negative traits, and second, argues for their integrative power in their capacity to compel submission from individuals. His account of his own education exemplifies this, and it is also evident in his fictional representation of the conflicts between the guardians of orthodoxy like Mr Poon, and marginals like Wallace Nolasco, or of the intransigence of a 'Chinese' purist like Lily Chen. Extending from this, the novels are often angled to show the power of established structures – which is also the power of un-reason and oppression – and its ultimate triumph over individual subjectivity through its capacity to co-opt, incorporate or exclude. We see this in the fortunes of Chase and Eastman, Adolph Ng and the cast of characters in *Brownout* and *Renegade or Halo*[2]. Thus the crux of the problem is Mo's conception of culture, of which the denigration of 'Chinese' culture and his self-exile from it offers an early and contentious demonstration. However, it is important to note that while this conception certainly informs the novels, and constitutes a recurrent narra-tive discourse, the discourse of cultures as structures of power is also complicated and challenged in Mo's work. For instance, Chinese ethnicity and culture, rather than the product of a single character's or narrator's point of view, are refracted through the prism of shifting perspectives. Mo's public state-ments and quarrels, while symptomatic of the structural approach to culture in his novels, do not do full justice to his fictional diagnoses and explorations. This discontinuity is itself a phenomenon worth reflecting on, in the sociology of writing in Britain today.

Though vocal about the characteristics of 'Chinese' culture, Mo seems to consider as self-evident what 'Britishness' is or entails. As I have discussed earlier, Mo calling himself 'a Brit' is inextricable from his denial of the 'Chinese' labelling; 'British' is the positive term against the negative term, 'Chinese', in the binary opposition that Mo constructed. The same, in a way, is true of the novels in which there are no 'British' characters of note. 'British' life is noticeably absent from *Sour Sweet* and can only be inferred as what 'Chinese' life is not, and British imperialistic adventures in *An Insular Possession* are largely mediated through the oppositional vantages of Chase and Eastman's reports. Only in the most recent novel, *Renegade or*

Halo[2], is 'Britishness' embodied in characters distinctly virtuous in themselves and as a function of difference from a seriously degraded world.

A more fruitful discussion is possible if we approach the question of Mo's 'Britishness' in terms of an affiliation to a literary tradition. In 'One of Billy's Boys', the identification, through his boxing-master, of combat and fiction is explicit, and given a characteristic farcical twist: '[Mr Tingle] looked, in 1957, much like a spry, elderly, weight-trained and cross-countried version of that other Billy, Bunter.'[22] 'Fighting their Writing' mentions a number of authors whose works – which might be seen as more robust versions of Billy Bunter's frolics – mark Mo's early reading, or make up what he calls 'a romantic literary culture' underpinning the 'stern code' of Mr Tingle, his boxing instructor (303). Chief among them is Robert Louis Stevenson whom Mo, following Graham Greene, rates highly as 'a master of descriptive action' (303). Using this as a yardstick, he gives a focused discussion of writing on fighting, and judges selected works by Hazlitt, Shaw and Thackeray to be less accomplished than those of a 'comparatively mediocre' writer, R. M. Ballantyne (303). Vivid and accurate description of action has to be accompanied by analysis, and this in turn requires powers of observation; on this score, Mo puts John Masefield 'on a par' with Hemingway, who, along with another lesser-known writer, James Jones, are the only exceptions in what he considers as an otherwise impoverished American writing on 'fisticuffs' (305).

Mo's references are largely British, and in naming them, he constructs a literary tradition and places himself as writer in it. It is a tradition which embraces his own passions for fighting and writing, offers models of narrative in which kinetic and verbal languages can be articulated, and lessons in craftsmanship so that he can write about the fight with passion. Through comparisons within the tradition, he develops critical judgement of what is 'good' from the 'less successful' in the craft of description and narrative. This rather specialised tutelage in the art of fiction develops a broader but related dimension when Mo calls up another list of writers from the popular tradition to accompany those mentioned earlier who might be seen to belong to a more exclusively literary culture. The second list includes Captain W. E. Johns, G. A. Henty, Percy F. Westerman, Leslie Charteris and Anthony Hope – fairly standard reading for boys of Mo's generation and class. Mo's fond memories of the 'derring-do' stories of Biggles, the Saint and the Prisoner of Zenda tell a story of a child reader which complements and completes the image of the idiosyncratic and combat-obsessed adult reader and writer. Together, the two lists enact the transition from an early identity formed by a received literary tradition to adult self-making – both as individual and writer – through selective reading choices. In this respect, 'Fighting their Writing' is a highly crafted and crafty act of self-fashioning, an invention of tradition which is at the same time a performance of the process of identity.

Mo's inventions of tradition and self are indubitably masculine, and for that, frankly conventional and stereotypical. The active life, defined by adventure and physical exploits, and the training of the body in order to live that life to the full, are central to this masculine tradition, from Henty and Haggard to Buchan and Hope. Heroism is the ethical mission, and combat the key to individual progress; community is usually male community, made up of friendships between men, bonded by the inalienable cause of biology and the inherited rights of class, tightened and undergirded by reticent but intensely held beliefs in the 'honour' of being 'British'.[23] Such is the uncomplicated and formulaic logic of the Biggles narratives, but Mo obviously delights in the ambivalence when this logic is rehearsed but also caricatured in Billy Bunter, Flashman and, to an extent, in the Saint. The performance of masculinity and its antithesis, the mock-heroic, are crucial perspectives on Mo's own fictional protagonists, especially Wallace Nolasco, Adolph Ng, Rey Castro in *Renegade or Halo²* and Lily Chen who was brought up like a boy by her father. A gendered reading of Mo's novels would find little that is innovative in their representation of heterosexual relations. With the nebulous exception of Lily – and her lesser literary cousin, Victoria Init in *Brownout* – his women characters are overshadowed by the men, pallid and unformed in the dominant discourse of masculinity and its absurd self-deflations.

Rather than his protagonists, it is in his descriptions and narratives that Mo best complicates the basic formula of masculine discourse enshrined in his early reading. 'Fighting their Writing' gives some sense of the concentration with which he honed his descriptive skills, and the tireless work on detail – his forte as a writer – is evident everywhere in the fight scenes and scenes of action in his novels – the hockey match in Part Two of *The Monkey King*, the bloody triad fights in *Sour Sweet*, the battles between the British and Chinese militia in *An Insular Possession*, the guerrilla war in *Redundancy* and the violent gang fights in *Brownout* and *Renegade or Halo²*. Mo's skills go beyond the description of action; the attention to myriad details and their co-ordination enable the spectacular realist tapestry of the Pearl River unfolded at the beginning of *An Insular Possession*, and the almost photographic sequences of the fall of Danu in *Redundancy*. It is one of the fascinating dualities of Mo as writer that the valorisation and parody of the restless energies of the 'masculine' go hand in hand with a patient and at times laborious focus on a meticulous realist art. 'What is more tedious than novel-writing?' Mo asks, 'Most weeks are just monotonous isolation in the big house.'[24] In this light, 'Fighting their Writing' takes on another meaning: the struggles of the writer against his own creative drive and its demands upon his time and endurance. It resonates, in another martial and prosaic key, of T. S. Eliot's 'intolerable wrestle with language' (*Four Quartets*).

Though stylistically different, and writing from different junctures of British imperialist history, three of the writers on Mo's reading list, Stevenson, Kipling and Graham Greene are all marked by the fascination with the foreign. Adventure, in their fiction, is framed by departure from the familiar milieu of middle-class British culture for uncharted territories, contact with alien subjects, and the opportunities this provides for self- and cultural reflection. The fact that in such fiction, the place of constant reference, whether conscious or unconscious, is the 'home' terrain of middle-class Britain; the fact that contact with others can never, even with the best of intentions, be entirely free from the desires, anxieties and pathologies of British imperialist will – these are textual undercurrents that have been much investigated in recent work on colonial discourse inspired by Edward Said's *Orientalism* and *Culture and Imperialism*.[25] Thus, for Mo to derive his literary parentage from these writers raises a question about the place of the imperial heritage and its narratives in his own sense of being 'British' – a question that has both political and aesthetic dimensions. It is a question to which I will return in the discussion of the novels in the following chapters.

Mo is acutely aware of his own situation as a 'British' writer in a postcolonial literary landscape. In an interview, he says, 'We live, especially in England, in the age of the end of empire... I think people like Rushdie and myself would have been joke figures in Kipling, if we got into Kipling. You know, *educated natives*.'[26] This affiliation for Rushdie, and the awareness that he is writing against a literature of empire which Kipling represents, take us back to the issue which I raised at the beginning of this introduction, of Mo's situation among other postcolonial writers of world literature. Mo as writer has taken up a mimetic challenge which also confronts many other postcolonial writers at the beginning of their careers: how to represent an indigenous, non-English, and former colonial society and culture in the English language. Taking up this challenge entails negotiations with the literary inheritance of English writing as it is embodied in those authors whose use of genres and traditions offers strategic inspiration in the writers' development of their own craft. Some twenty years before *The Monkey King*, Chinua Achebe effectively inaugurated postcolonial fiction with his exploration of the impact and the aftermath of colonialism in an African country. But he did so in two novels whose titles and subject matter declare a relationship to a tradition of western literary modernism: *Things Fall Apart*, a quotation from Yeats's 'The Second Coming', narrates the fragmentation of a native culture under colonialism, and *No Longer at Ease* (1960), a quotation from Eliot's 'The Journey of the Magi', speaks of a disillusionment after the failure of the utopianist project of the nation-state. Achebe's novels, up to and including parts of *Anthills of the Savannah* (1987), are also written as realist narratives, in the tradition of nineteenth-century European fiction, and this literary inheritance can be seen everywhere in Achebe's detailed account of Igbo, and Nigerian, daily life and social relations in his novels. Mo writes from a different set of preoccupations in which the cause of nationhood which inspired Achebe is noticeably absent but, like Achebe, he draws upon both realist and modernist traditions, mediated by English, in his fictions of Chinese family and culture, and this continues as he moves away from specifically Chinese subject matter.

There are, however, non-literary or specifically political dimensions to writing in English, for the language and the literary traditions it inscribes are often seen as legacies of colonialism, thus rendering its use particularly problematic – or even inappropriate – for representing societies and communities deeply marked by colonialism, or formed out of the fight against it. English has become the crux of linguistic and political struggles in many former colonies of the British empire, and with the migrations from the former colonies, has doubled back on Britain itself. Achebe himself has been attacked by other African writers for his use of English, and has eloquently defended his choice.[27] But the controversy over English continues to shadow postcolonial writers. More recently, speaking of the use of English for Indian themes, Rushdie says,

> we can't simply use the language in the way the British did; that it needs remaking for our own purposes. Those of us who do use English do so in spite of our ambiguity towards it, or perhaps because of that, perhaps because we can find in that linguistic struggle a reflection of other struggles taking place in the real world, struggles between the cultures within ourselves and the influences at work upon our societies. To conquer English may be to complete the process of making ourselves free.

As for the British dimension of the struggle, Rushdie continues, 'the British Indian writer simply does not have the option of rejecting English, anyway... in the forging of a British Indian identity the English language is of central importance'.[28] The conflict over English, as Rushdie suggests, is one site of ongoing cultural contestations which constitute writers like him as subjects, fuel the dynamic of change within their different cultures of belonging, and create a bond of community – the 'we' of the quotation – between writers from dispersed global locations. In this conflict, Rushdie differentiates between English as a mark of colonial subjection, and the radical import in the writers' adoption and ownership of the language as they remake it in their own images and their representations of reality and history.

Mo has not really addressed the issue of English as directly or as publicly as the other writers, and his predominantly realist strategies clearly depart from the dream narratives and magic realism of Rushdie's novels.[29] But there are broad lines of agreement between them, not least in their similar positioning as 'ethnic' writers on the British literary landscape. Recently, when asked why he chose to write about Chinese characters despite his professed ignorance and dislike of Chinese culture, Mo replied that 'it's mainly because in the tradition of English literature, there are very few Chinese characters. Many Indians, yes, but Chinese are rare.'[30] Besides an engagement in the literary practice and politics of English, Mo shares with Rushdie a common interest in what the latter describes as 'other struggles taking place in the real world, struggles between the cultures within ourselves and the influences at work upon our societies.' A countercultural sensibility characterises their work, specifically in their fictional critiques of the orthodox and boundary-forming tendencies in traditional cultures that are buttressed by the realities of power and oppression. Both writers perform the role of cultural iconoclasts, their stock-in-trade that of the satirist, irreverent, ironic, mocking, and it is this investment in satire which distinguishes the novels of both from the work of Achebe. But while Rushdie places a premium on cross-cultural hybridity both in his fiction and essays, Mo's novels show a much greater hesitation about the hybrid as the agent of historical change, whether in local situations or in what he calls 'the clash of inimical civilisations'.[31] This expression is Mo's shorthand for a perspective on culture which stresses opposition and conflict as the norm of cultural encounters, and the contest for dominance between cultures as the ineluctable dynamic of history. Mo's creative sympathies lie with those individuals and communities caught in the conflict, who cannot or refuse to remake themselves in the images of domination, who try to build their own bridge to history, and fall, tragically and invariably, into the interstices.

In recent years, Mo has sought to distance himself from writers of his generation including Rushdie and William Boyd whose fiction ranges far beyond the domestic dramas and national boundaries of Britain. Instead, he expresses recurrent admiration for the work and example of V. S. Naipaul. It is hardly surprising that Mo should feel an attraction for Naipaul, not least because of their common proclivity for the controversial, especially in their attitudes towards the developing world or so-called Third World. Though his views on the degradation of the Third World are robustly stated, Naipaul's fiction and travel writing show an intellectual complexity which Mo's work has yet to achieve. Mo has real strengths in setting a scene, and in extricating drama from the ordinary and unremarkable. His protagonists have many sides to them which make them fascinating in themselves, but as social and cultural observers, they too often fall back on reductive stereotyping which reveals their intellectual limitations. In a self-conscious essay on the art of narrating, Naipaul reviews his choice of narrator for an account of a journey:

> The narrator is going up a highland river in an unnamed South American country. Who is this narrator? What can he be made to be? This is often where fiction can simply become false.
>
> To make the narrator a writer or traveller would be true to the actual experience; but then the fictional additions would be quite transparent. Can the narrator be a man in disguise, a man on the run?...

> A man on the run would have been true to the place.
> But narrative has its own strictness. It requires pertinence
> at all times, and to have given that character to the
> narrator would have introduced something not needed, a
> distraction, something that wouldn't have tied up with
> what was to come at the end of his journey.[32]

Naipaul turns the occasion of beginning his own story into a
meta-discourse on narrative, drawing up rules about what is or
what is not appropriate without, however, losing sight of the
task at hand. This is just one small instance of Naipaul's ability
to resolve the abstract and the actual into each other which is
everywhere evident in his work.

Mo appears to have learnt one aspect of the lesson from
Naipaul, especially in his first-person narrators like Adolph Ng
and Rey Castro; they are always 'pertinent', or true to the
ordinariness in which Mo has cast them. But the restricted
intellectual scope – without what Naipaul calls 'fictional addi-
tions' – which Mo allows them actually diminishes their character,
and draws in the horizons of their narrative. The novels they are
in talk of war, the national and global, conflicts within and
between cultures. Perfectly capable in describing these epical
themes as day-to-day experiences, they are inapt when it comes
to resolving experiences as ideas so as to give their narrative a
finer, more intricate texture. And in first-person narratives,
there is little that is not inflected by the one voice, in its silences
as much as its nuances. Curiously, in the novels narrated in the
third person, the narrative perspective is often hostage to its
focalisation through the protagonists. Thus when the characters
are more actors than thinkers, like the Filipino characters in
Brownout, the third-person narrator rarely supplements with
comments on what their thoughtlessness has caused them to
misconstrue, or simply to miss, in regard to the significance and
implications of their situation; indeed *Brownout*, with its stringent observations about an academic conference, is the most
self-consciously anti-intellectual of Mo's novels. The domestic
worlds of Wallace and Lily may not be the 'natural' domain of
the intellect, and as the third-person narrator shows, a non-

reflexive habit of mind is actually a virtue and an asset for both of them. But in Mo's epical turns towards the historical and the global, the scenes and events which he engages with – often densely observed – demand not only a multivocal and knowing narrator – which he also fashions – but also a finely-tuned intellect capable of realising the grandeur of ideas and beliefs that drive human history, and can grasp the abstract in the quotidian. In this light, among Mo's protagonists, it is Gideon Chase in *An Insular Possession*, whose scholarly sobriety best approaches the contemplative and reflexive; he is, however, a lone voice not only in the novel he inhabits, but also in the world of Mo's novels populated by characters who live the drama of action rather than the drama of intellect. The fact that he is neither comic in himself, nor the cause of mirth in others confirms how much he goes against the grain of Mo's talent.

The Chinese family at home:
The Monkey King

*T*HE *Monkey King*, Timothy Mo's first novel, was published in 1978, but the story is set more than two decades earlier, at the time of Mo's own childhood in Hong Kong.[1] Mo was able, as he acknowledged in the brief preface, to draw upon his 'personal knowledge' in writing the novel. This insider claim is immediately qualified by the admission that as author, his 'personal knowledge' can only be partial, and needed to be supplemented by 'sociological and anthropological studies' so as to 'keep the colonial background as accurate as possible'. There are other reasons why it is misleading to read the novel as an insider's narrative about 'the Chinese'. *The Monkey King* is located specifically in the Cantonese family and culture of mid-century colonial Hong Kong, and although Cantonese and Chinese are interchangeable terms in the novel, it does not present itself as a trans-historical and pan-ethnic portrait of Chinese culture. That the main characters think, speak and act as indisputable authorities on 'Chinese' culture is actually a target of the novel's satire.

The novel begins in Macau,[2] the Portuguese colony close to Hong Kong. Rather than starting with a description of landscape or a catalogue of geographical minutiae, Mo establishes the place of the novel by focusing on the ethnic relations between a Macanese like Wallace Nolasco, who has Portuguese ancestry, and the Cantonese majority. As the novel opens, Mo tells how a history of contact between Chinese and Portuguese on the periphery of empire has produced a racially mixed population living in close proximity, 'cheek by jaundiced jowl' (3). Though of Portuguese descent, a character like Wallace has become physically indistinguishable from the Chinese, and spoke 'impeccable Cantonese'. But this objective reality of racial and linguistic identification seems invisible to the characters themselves, and is consciously denied by them. Wallace, for instance, 'affected not to understand that vulgar, braying dialect' of the Cantonese (3),[3] and draws a deliberate linguistic boundary to separate himself off from the majority population. This is self-distinction in another sense, for Wallace clearly sees himself as superior, a perception which the Chinese, equally segregationist and culturally supremacist, return in kind. The basic comic premise, then, is the dealings of two parties each unshakeably convinced of their manifest superiority to each other.[4]

From time to time, the thought of affiliation with the Chinese breaks through in Wallace's consciousness but is immediately pushed aside, disparaged as the aberration of 'fanciful moments', and an intolerable bond of constriction – he can only imagine himself and the Chinese 'as prisoners together in a long chain-gang'(3). Such is the ethno-cultural location of Mo's fictional 'Macau', and later 'Hong Kong', where the objective and observable reality of commonality is denied subjectively by the characters who continue to think of and see each other as being on opposing sides of an ethnic and linguistic divide, and to enforce strictly drawn social boundaries. From this initial confrontation, the characters move, by fits and starts, towards a particular kind of accommodation as the drama of the novel unfolds within the time-frame stretching from the 1950s to the early 1970s.

The Monkey King has a tripartite structure. Part One focuses on Wallace's life, as son-in-law, in the arcane corridors of the Poon family, his struggles against the authority of the patriarch, Mr Poon, and his attempts at rebellion. Part Two narrates his exile with his wife, May Ling, to a rural village in Hong Kong, and his transformation there into community leader and entrepreneur. Part Three concludes with his return and his triumphal succession to Mr Poon as patriarch and head of the family business. The narrative interweaves a number of different but also related strands in Mo's literary inheritance. Read as the story of the fortunes of a young man who sets out in an unfamiliar world with little to rely on except his native wit, and wins in the end after fending off the numerous attacks of an arch-opponent or his minions, *The Monkey King* is an adult, and artistically accomplished, rehearsal of the adventure stories of Mo's childhood reading. In his seminal work, *Anatomy of Criticism*, Northrop Frye states: 'The theme of the comic is the integration of society, which usually takes the form of incorporating a central character in it... The obstacles to the [comic] hero's desire ... form the action of the comedy, and the overcoming of them the comic resolution. The obstacles are usually parental, hence comedy often turns on a clash between a son's and a father's will.'[5] The traditional contours of comedy, as they are charted by Frye, are clearly visible – and domesticated – in Mo's novel, in the character of Wallace, the inter-generational conflict between the younger protagonist and older patriarch, and its resolution. From a third vantage, the passage of Wallace from social marginal to the centre of a fictional establishment of power and authority can also be mapped onto the progress of the *picaro* in a literary classic like Henry Fielding's *Tom Jones*.

These intertextual references to European generic types enter into dialogue with those to the classic Chinese narrative, *The Journey to the West* (Hsi-yu Chi),[6] an allegorical fantasy, steeped in Buddhist doctrine, about the pilgrimage of a monk and his disciples in search of the holy scriptures. The leading disciple, Monkey, is a hybrid of simian and human natures, an expert both in the martial and magical arts who can metamorphose into myriad other inanimate or creatural forms. He begins as a minor god in his own right, ruling over a kingdom of monkeys, but falls into disgrace when his animal nature prevails and he becomes an anarchic trouble-maker and rebel of the Buddhist divine order. Subdued by the holy monk and converted to Buddhism, he accompanies his master on the perilous pilgrimage. The journey is both punitive and redemptive; he has to battle numerous demons along the way, and in successfully

discussion/interaction between Western + Chinese lit tradition

triumphing over them and protecting his master, is allowed to return to the divine fold at the end. Monkey's magical powers of disguise and self-transformation are reined in, literally and symbolically, through the golden band placed on his head by the monk; at moments on the journey when he strains against his master's authority, the band induces searing headaches which only the master's special chanting can relieve. As both fictional character and an ethnic 'Chinese' archetype, the Monkey King is a transgressor moving between heaven and earth, the spirit and the human world, authority and its discontents.[7] He is polytropic, resourceful and agile, a trickster, rebel and comic hero, but his transgressive individualism is ultimately contained within the rules of an established teleological structure to the end of strengthening both in a bond of mutual benefit. In the guise of comic fantasy and religious allegory, *The Journey to the West* inscribes a particular Chinese transaction between selfhood and society. Through Wallace and his adventures, Mo relocates this legendary model of selfhood and society in the modern colonial periphery. In his resistance against the authority of Mr Poon, and his multiple transformations, Wallace is the eponymous Monkey King.

Animating the comic discourse in these literary antecedents – both west and east – is the energy of youthful rebellion. Though mindful of the stresses and strains such energy can generate, comedy works towards its accommodation within existing social order, and its value in enlarging social sympathies and social renewal. In theorising the paradigms of traditional comedy, Frye has observed, 'At the beginning … the forces thwarting the hero are in control of [the narrative's] society, but … The action of the comedy moves towards the incorporation of the hero into the society that he naturally fits.'[8] The narrative of Mo's novel shows the rebel and his adversaries engaging in a continuous match of wit and stratagem. In the course of this engagement, both sides develop the qualities of flexibility and tolerance on which their eventual accommodation will rest. At the end of the novel, social order remains intact but in a different configuration from that at the beginning. While the younger protagonist moves from outsider to being a valued member of the establishment, the inherited hierarchies of power and intra-cultural antagonisms also give way to a new and more inclusive sociality. What we witness in *The Monkey King* is the progressive erosion of those ethnic and cultural boundaries which mark off Wallace from the Cantonese, and them from him. Initially conflictual, Wallace's relations with Mr Poon and the Poon family develop into an uneasy truce in the course of the first part of the novel, and later on, to a new re-identification. The Poon family is mobilised and rejuvenated by the injection of Wallace's ex-centric vitality, and Wallace, in turn, liberalises the hierarchical order of the family, and releases the natural bond of kinship into the flow of reciprocal sympathies. But as we shall see, a darker undercurrent flows beneath this social resolution; there is a psychological price to be paid as Wallace's subjectivity and the culture of the family are simultaneously reconstituted. In a moment of gothic terror at the end, the narrative breaks its dominant realist mode, and deconstructs its comic closure.

Soon after the opening, the geographical setting shifts from 'Macau' to 'Hong Kong', but the same ethnic boundaries pertain to the British as to the Portuguese colony. Wallace's marriage to May Ling is one of convenience. Mr Poon, whose wealth and extensive business interests remain very much a mystery to his immediate family, requires a husband for a daughter who suffers the disadvantage of being the offspring of a minor concubine and, without claims to a substantial dowry, an unattractive marriage prospect to any self-respecting Chinese man. 'Under the circumstances,' the narrator observes drily, 'a poor Portuguese was a creative solution.' And as Mr Poon calculates:

> It would be possible to economise on the initial capital outlay of the dowry to balance out defrayments on an additional mouth. Wallace might also have his uses in certain business projects Mr Poon had in mind. And while not a celestial, Wallace was not a real *faan gwai lo*, a foreign devil. Compromise was at the centre of Mr Poon's political system, and in securing Wallace he had achieved such a balance. (8)

The quotation resonates with the satiric tenor which characterises the novel. Entering into Mr Poon's frame of mind, the narrator sketches the outlines of a man as auditing mechanism whose rhythms of thought seem to move as rapidly and fluently as fingers over a Chinese abacus. In Mr Poon's material scheme of things, Wallace figures merely as a disembodied 'additional mouth', and their prospective familial relations are delimited as those between consumer and provider, which are further subject to the principle of use value. But true to the Dickensian grotesque of which this caricature is a successor, Mr Poon's outrageous calculation, with its additional accounting of racial prejudice against Wallace – 'not a celestial' – are stated in the flattest, most matter-of-fact tone of voice. As the calculations draw to a close, Mr Poon's self-congratulatory voice is doubled with the disingenuous praise of the narrator-as-satirist. The final sentence mocks its own subject, but it is possible also to detect in the mockery a sneaking admiration for Mr Poon's adroit management of the demands of both practical necessity and ethnic and cultural prejudices.

In the novel, Mr Poon interiorises a complex exchange of patriarchal, materialistic and political forces which determine his self-identity and sociality. As caricature, which is what we see in the above quotation, he appears both monstrous and ludicrously simple; elsewhere in the novel, he is a much more shadowy figure. Taking his first tentative steps into Mr Poon's byzantine scheme of things, Wallace, with the patriarch's arm around him in a gesture of masculine kinship and patronage, is led down an unlit corridor stacked on both sides with old newspapers leading to a cluttered table where the old man does his accounts. Decrepitude and decay are Mr Poon's favoured disguise, and the gloom and disarray of his physical surroundings convey the impression of an animal in his lair to which the unsuspecting Wallace is gently lured. As the novel proceeds and the focus of the narrative shifts to Wallace and his antics, Mr Poon recedes further from view and appears, in Wallace's occasional encounters with him, as secretive and verbally reticent, speaking in riddles about his actions and plans. Seen through the eyes of

Wallace, the mystery of Mr Poon reflects back on Wallace's own *naïveté* and continued exclusion in his adopted 'home'. But both Wallace and the narrator can see how Mr Poon's control is felt by every member of the family. Like a ghostly presence, or an ancestral tradition, his authority is immanent in the miserly regime he has set up in the household, and the competition for material comforts that it encourages among the family members. They are bonded to him by a common recognition of his will and power as provider, and a submission both unthinking and habitual. Outside the family, the novel recurrently hints at, but never makes clear, his influence in the community, and the network of obligations and patronage on which this influence is based and through which it is disseminated.

'When I think of the realist tradition in fiction,' Raymond Williams once wrote, 'I think of the kind of novel which creates and judges the quality of a whole way of life in terms of the qualities of persons.'[9] What then is 'the way of life' which the novel 'creates and judges' through Mr Poon? As a shadowy manipulator, he embodies the conservative and centrifugal forces which structure the family as an inherited institution, and which are held in place by covert strategies of cohesion. What pertains within the family is replicated, again through Mr Poon, in communal bonds premised on inequities of wealth, age and ethnic origins. These enact the novel's substantive and riotous critique of 'Chinese' culture, and it is also at this juncture that two further questions can be raised.[10]

The first has to do with the slippages between 'Cantonese' and 'Chinese' which occur throughout the novel so that the fiction of a specific geographical and ethnic location comes to stand for an entire and complex configuration of cultures. This is a question which is germane not only to *The Monkey King* but also later on to *Sour Sweet*, because of the paucity of fictional discourse on the 'Chinese' in contemporary British literature with which Mo's novels can enter into dialogue. In this lack, an illusion of these novels' representativeness, as evident in the reviews, takes shape, which Mo's own artistic accomplishments and public polemic no doubt help, and will continue, to perpetuate.

A critical reading practice will therefore need to construe the novels in an emerging genealogy of 'Chineseness' in Britain, both in fiction and other cultural documents as they become available, and will also need to be alert to the destabilisations of Mo's mimesis.

The other and outstanding ethical question in the critique hangs on Mr Poon's motives, and in implicitly addressing this question, the novel's satiric antipathy is counterbalanced by its comic drives towards social resolution. It is a balance achieved by alternating a number of perspectives on Mr Poon: largely unseen by Wallace at the beginning, he is the looming tyrant, and takes the blame for Wallace's material privation and alienation in the latter's reckoning. But he also shows no rancour or vindictiveness when Wallace challenges his authority on a number of occasions. This ambivalence is amplified when Wallace increasingly comes to see him as the paternal benefactor whose self-interest is actually an investment in the survival and interest of the family as a whole. Whether this transformation in Wallace's viewpoint points to what Mr Poon really is, or just to his son-in-law's gradual incorporation into the ideology and culture of the family, is left very much open to question. In this respect, there are really no stable ethical conclusions to be drawn in Mo's representation of 'Chinese' family and culture.

Besides Wallace's relationship with Mr Poon, Part One also gives us numerous vignettes of his encounters with the other family members. In its narrative of the Poon family – its hierarchies, rituals and everyday life – the novel looks, at times, quasi-anthropological. But unlike Achebe's *Things Fall Apart* where whole chapters are given over to accounts of pre-colonial Igbo festivals and rituals from what appears to be the perspective of a knowledgeable insider, the anthropological impulse in *The Monkey King* serves its dominant satiric orientation. As the narrative delves into the Poons' daily life, the Chinese family takes shape less as an integrated structure than as the cloister of the idiosyncratic and the bizarre, the mean and the venial. Mo astutely exploits his own knowledge and experience of the Chinese family, but in making the satiric observations from the viewpoint of Wallace, the alien from another culture, Mo also deactivates possible connections between his fictional use of his own knowledge and insider claims. The reader sees the Poon family through the eyes of an outsider; and as the narrative unfolds, it is through Wallace's experience of being kept in his place by the other members as they assert their seniority and prior belonging, that the interior hierarchies of the family are gradually revealed with a horrible comic relish.

Like initiates into an alien culture, Wallace – and the reader – observes some of the stranger rituals of behaviour in the Poon family. A number of these initial encounters revolve around food and the way it is served and consumed; Wallace, as an 'additional mouth', is, of course, a very interested party. In the following passage, he is stopped short by the sight of how a new 'mouth' is fed:

> The amahs … were dropping morsels into the child's mouth from their chopsticks. They first took a tit-bit from the dish and put it in their own mouths, masticating slowly and thoroughly. Then the mashed nourishment would be shaped into a ball by rolling it with the tip of the tongue against the barrier of the front teeth. The amahs forced the food out through pursed lips, gathered it in their plastic pincers and transferred the pre-masticated pellet into the child's mouth.
>
> He almost forgot what he had come to tell May Ling. (12)

Wallace's gaze is transfixed by this process of feeding which can also be seen as a metonym for cultural transmission within the family. He is immobilised and passive, with no will of his own, very much like the child who is being fed, and this, in turn, suggests his initial place in the family as its latest newcomer. Earlier on, the reader is told how 'the servants held the household to ransom' (11) by withholding all but the worst food from those lowly members in the family hierarchy who include May Ling, sons- or daughters-in-law like Wallace, and minor dependants like the child who is the son of May Ling's mother, a lesser concubine, from another marriage. Here, in the passage, we can see how the servants have refined the rituals of food and familial culture into a precise, almost industrial art. Dispensing titbits and morsels, they implement the carefully planned economy of Mr Poon's regime, and in the masticating, mashing, and ejecting of food like 'pellets' through 'the barrier of the front teeth', mimic his aggressive calculation. There is something both comical and sinister about this, a mixture of fascination and repulsion to which Wallace's momentary state of shock wordlessly attests. He is the voyeur of an unfamiliar and bizarre ritual but what is emblematised in this *mise en scène* is also his own abjection as witless captive of the functionaries in the Poon hierarchy.

Shortly after, Wallace notices that the ritual of feeding has stopped, and on pressing his inquiries as to the child's whereabouts, finds the family evasive and embarrassed until, 'via circumlocution and euphemism' (16), he finally manages to extract a vague reply from Mr Poon that the child is dead and buried. The narrator never explicitly identifies Wallace and the child, but in an outstanding example of indirection, draws cross-references between the sinister fate of the hapless child and the precariousness of Wallace's situation. Through a succession of images, both striking and poignant, the novel offers a glimpse of its anti-comic discourse, its awareness not only of the indignities of the dependent body but life devalued in the family's submission to an unquestioned established order. In the final moments of the incident, Wallace sees the box the child used to sleep in outside the door of the reception room, ready to be taken away. Subsuming and extending his point of view, the narrator describes knowingly what can be seen through the open balcony of the room: kites, flying high above the tenement buildings, their thick strings visible, 'climbing jerkily until brought up at the end of their tether' (16). For a while, they remain in tension until their strings snap, and the narrator can see a litter of wrecked kites on the telegraph poles. He continues:

> There was one in the nullah. The remnants of its broken string had snagged on tins at the edge of the sluggish

trickle of water. Rubbish floated by, including a bloated dog, its belly so distended its legs seemed like the teats of a monstrous udder. The carcass circled in a murky whirlpool, then spun off at a tangent towards a mud bank in the centre of the nullah. At the last moment it was swept off into one of the forks of deeper water on each side and disappeared into the tunnel under the road and, eventually, the harbour. (16)

Funerals are expensive. The fate of the body is never made explicit, but the metaphorical import of the images of the kite and the dog's carcass in the nullah, or dry riverbed, is unmistakable. They co-ordinate to form the habitat of family and community as one of physical degradation and death, a naturalised environment unnoticed by Wallace or any of the characters. The discourse of the narrator contains a much more critical indictment of the family and its culture than the non-self-reflexive actions and experiences of the characters would allow. As the novel develops, what distinguishes Wallace from the other characters is a subjectivity in which momentary surfacings of the unconscious question – without really disrupting – his comic trajectory.

The need to feed and his body's discomfort preoccupy Wallace during his period of initiation into the Poon household. Despite his meagre diet, Wallace remains observant, his senses alert, as he trains his body to adapt to and survive the mealtime routines: 'Wallace ... knew when to anticipate food because the servants ... warm[ed] it up exactly three minutes before they served the dishes, the period, as he discovered by experiment, that he could go without breathing. By the time his face had mottled, he knew it was time to go in. Dizziness did not seem to impair his appetite and certainly, as he found out early on, it was fatal to be late' (13). The family meal, as Wallace quickly realises, is a constant Malthusian struggle for inadequate resources, where dishes are served 'at a signal from Mr Poon'; those 'currently in favour with [him] ... could ... hope for a sliver of marrow shaved off the sides', and only the patriarch, lord of the food chain, gets enough and can 'pull his chair back, belching contentedly' at the end, leaving the others 'with a sense of anti-climax' and Wallace himself 'staring wistfully at the gleaming plates' (14).

Training his own satirical eye on the family hierarchy, Wallace disdains most of the competition and backbiting among the other members which Mr Poon's stingy resource allocation encourages. Instead, the novel's comic *agon* pitches him directly against the old man in two early acts of mock-heroic insurrection in which the body's discomforts – his own and others' – are again writ large (Chapter 3). Unable to bear the chilly damp of the Poon house any longer, Wallace makes a clandestine trip to the local market, and returns with some faggots which he tries to light in the fireplace in the reception room with newspapers from Mr Poon's stacks, without knowing that the old man has stashed gold ingots up the chimney. This quest for fire develops a quasi-Promethean note because it is unsanctioned and moreover, is a direct threat to the source of patriarchal power. Then in rapid succession, Wallace is transformed from classical rebel to modern revolutionary when he physically intervenes to stop Mr Poon from a savage beating of the eldest son, Ah Lung, who, in the patriarchal scheme of things, bullies his sisters and servants but cringes before his father's power. In the heat of the moment, Wallace rounds on Mr Poon: 'You couldn't behave like this in the modern ages. You thought you was the God of us all or something? ... You would never oppress anybodys with that again' (21). From covert and self-defensive action to direct challenge – Wallace's rapid self-transformations rehearse the simian agility of the Monkey King in straining against the socio-cultural orthodoxies which hold him in his place.

But just as every small act of rebellion on the part of the Monkey King marks another step towards his assigned place in a preordained divine scheme, the first part of Mo's novel also witnesses Wallace's gradual, and unwitting, incorporation into Mr Poon's personal and familial designs. The passion of youthful rebellion can hardly sustain itself when the asymmetries of economic power overwhelmingly favour the scheming will of old age. This sobering cultural perception runs counter to the comic *agon* of this and later novels, and is complicated by the exclusions which Wallace already suffers as an ethnic marginal and outsider to the family. Wallace attempts to form an alliance with his wife, May Ling; for her, it is gender rather than ethnic inequality which combines with inherited family hierarchy to inhibit both personal expression and response to Wallace's conjugal and political overtures. She is mostly silent, and when she speaks, can muster only isolated sounds and sentences. At the same time, she is discomfited by his attempts at greater intimacy between them, and would rather be left alone. In the following quotation, the personal and the cultural are imbricated through a blending of May Ling's point of view with that of the implied narrator: 'This was more; it amounted to a systematic attempt to destroy her points of reference and stability, leaving her at the mercy of the prevailing current of barbarian culture, in the sure knowledge that if it did not sweep her into her husband's arms, fright would' (36). We hear not only the voice of May Ling speaking from the heart of personal anxiety and ethnic prejudice but also the familiar amusement of the narrator as the sardonic observer of character and culture. The latter continues: 'The family resisted it as such. Any change Wallace brought about in May Ling would impinge directly on them; it would affect them more than May Ling. She had never existed as more than the aggregate of their joint expectations. To change one aspect of her personality was to destroy one of her functions in the household. And their very menialness made their loss the more acute' (36). May Ling, to put it simply, has no character to speak of; she is entirely the function of a woman in patriarchy and a member of an underclass in a centrifugal household. In the novel, she is a cipher of those socio-cultural forces which shape all the characters, and if she changes, or her position in the family improves, that is the measure of the changing situation of Wallace himself. Like the child in comparison with whose fate Wallace's experience appears as fortunate, May Ling's foil is the hapless Fong, Ah Lung's wife. Even the pathetic rebellion of Fong's suicide attempt is imprisoned in unchanging tradition, 'the conventional revenge of harassed daughters-in-law in olden China' (61). The novel's effervescent comedy and the narrator's engaging cynicism are shadowed by reminders of the rough justice which operates outside the narrative of social advancement, where the price of unbelonging and abjection can only be death.

In the remainder of the first part of the narrative, Wallace becomes the unwitting agent of Mr Poon's design to secure the finances, and thus the future, of the family dynasty. A position is found for Wallace in the Public Works Department where ostensibly he can put his training as an engineer to good use, and communicate with senior colonial civil servants, foreigners like himself. Mr Poon's secret game-plan is that Wallace will ingratiate himself with those in charge of construction contracts and become a channel by which these contracts, and the enormous profits they bring, will be given to the family business concern. While Mr Poon continues to scheme, the keynote of his character begins to shift from the tyrannical to the benevolent; at the same time, Wallace's perceived ethnic disadvantage becomes a business asset. These subtle changes destabilise the hierarchies within the family, and the ethnic boundaries that we have seen at the beginning.

There is a conspicuous difference as the narrative moves out of the claustrophobic family to 'Hong Kong' society. Through Wallace's contacts with his boss, Mr Allardyce, and Mabel, a friend and business partner of Mr Poon's, the novel paints a picture of colonial Hong Kong in the 1950s and 1960s as the habitat of eccentrics, corruptible but jovial civil servants, and women of dubious origins and repute who collude and socialise under the invisible aegis of Cantonese business interest. The representation is largely benign, and entirely in keeping with both the comic tenor of the novel and Mo's remembrances of his early life in Hong Kong which we have seen. At the same time, it draws attention to the multi-ethnic dimensions of Hong Kong society which have always co-existed with – and in parallel to – the mono-ethnic, Cantonese community organised around the family. The figure of Mabel is the enigmatic sign of the crossings between these two 'Hong Kongs'; a hybrid not unlike Wallace, she is marginalised from his narrative. The novel hints at, but never makes clear, a liaison between her and Mr Poon which, together with his choice and patronage of Wallace as son-in-law, suggest that out of his entirely pragmatic interests – or in the name of business – a culture in between the Cantonese and its expatriate and Eurasian others has been fostered. This is the culture which Mo himself embodies, and perhaps knows best, to judge from his memoirs of early childhood and the representation of 'Hong Kong' in *The Monkey King*. Textually, in both his memoirs and fiction – and memoir-writing, of course, involves fictionalisation – 'Hong Kong' is a 'frontier' in at least three senses of the word. First, it is a colony at the furthest reach of the British empire. This is an aspect of Hong Kong's history which Mo largely ignores in *The Monkey King* but will address in *An Insular Possession*. Second, it is the border between the Chinese-Cantonese and a variety of foreigners and others. Third, it is a social setting in which people of different cultural identities – however they are defined and expressed – deal with each other in an emerging community.

The substantial changes to Wallace's position, and his ultimate transformation from dependent subject to autonomous agent, do not begin until Part Two, in which he and May Ling leave the family and city for the country refuge in the rural New Territories. This journey – which is also an exile – is set in motion by a government investigation of the repair works on a construction site done by Mr Poon's firm, which collapse during a rainstorm. Mr Poon's culpability is not made clear at this point and certainly not to Wallace; in his apprehension about the investigation, Wallace gratefully clutches at the old man's offer of a getaway. The dependency in which Wallace is placed by his circumstances has become a condition of existence: 'As he was going, Mr Poon called out: "And Wallace." He turned obediently. "I don't think you knew how much our family were loving you." Wallace swallowed a lump. Through watery eyes he thought he saw a shadow or a small animal in the corridor. When he blinked there was nothing' (100). Wallace's surrender is symbolised in this uncanny moment at the end of Part One, set in that very corridor down which he is first led by Mr Poon. The voice of the patriarch, the superego, commands Wallace's unthinking obedience while his former self, like an elusive 'shadow' or 'small animal', lingers briefly on the edge of conscious recognition before being repressed, or pushed out of sight, by his quiescence to patriarchal and corporate desire. This is one way of seeing it; of course, what he glimpses in the corridor could equally well be a rat.

The pastoral turn in Part Two can be read in a number of ways. Arranged by Mr Poon, it starts out as a journey of regression for Wallace in which all residual traces of his resistant self are erased. But from the moment of arrival, pastoral exile takes shape as a journey of liberation: the byzantine corridors of the Poon mansion are left behind as Wallace and May Ling take a 'long, exhilarating walk' (106) in bucolic surroundings to the village. In this transition from Part One to Two, the novel rehearses both of the traditional comic forms identified by Frye: 'one is to throw the main emphasis on the blocking characters; the other is to throw it forward on the scenes of discovery and reconciliation. One is the general tendency of comic irony, satire, realism, and studies of manners; the other is the tendency of … romantic comedy.'[11] Without completely abandoning the first tendency, even though the 'blocking' character of Mr Poon is removed, Part Two also shows the growing bond between Wallace and May Ling in the pleasures of their rural retreat which, in the spirit of romantic comedy, promises a new and better family regime from the one under Mr Poon.

It is also significant that Mr Poon is not a native of the village but an outsider with property rights, rather like Wallace himself initially in the Poon household; thus Wallace is not being symbolically incorporated into the ancestral fold but released into an uncharted space with its opportunities for self-definition through adventure. Part Two begins by mapping this space geographically and anthropologically, making it known to Wallace and, through his and the narrator's vantages, to the readers. Through a number of crises, Wallace assumes the

mantle of entrepreneur and community leader; he successfully
transforms the village into a vacation destination for city-dwellers,
and resolves an ancient feud with a neighbouring village. Within the pastoral frame, the narratives of individual liberation and
progress intersect with that of colonial and capitalist modernity,
and in their complicated transactions, Mo relocates the dominant thematics of nineteenth and early twentieth-century
English realist fiction in a peripheral time and place.

The village's internal hierarchies are far less rigid than
those of the Poon household; Wallace and May Ling, as the most
recent arrivals, settle in quickly and with little trouble. But the
village also appears as much less than a pastoral idyll for it is the
site of inherited feuds and haunt of native superstition. A
fortuitous storm, which floods the paddy fields, enables Wallace
to take up the challenges of his new abode, and emerge, like 'a
snake shucking its skin' (133), from the role of infant dependant
to a full-grown agent. Combining his early training as an
engineer with daring ingenuity, he dynamites the sides of the
valley where the fields are, partially drains the flood waters, and
leaves behind a small lake which, in another inspired move, he
turns into a vacation site where people from the city can row and
fish. These ventures bring material improvement to the life of
the village, and Wallace demonstrates an imaginative realism
which matches Mr Poon's wit for the 'creative solution', and
proves him the old man's worthy heir. The village, his adopted
home – not unlike the Poon family – is remade in Wallace's
image as the site of play and profit, but while Mr Poon schemes,
Wallace improvises; consensual as he is convivial, he volunteers
his ideas as service to the community rather than as the route to
power.

The oppressive, wordless rituals of consumption which bind
the Poon family culture are displaced as new bonds of affiliation
are enacted which relocate Wallace and May Ling in an extended
village community and beyond that, to connections with other
ancestral communities in the pastoral order. Change is again the
keynote, and games, rather than rituals, signify a different
sociality. Wallace devises a quasi-hockey match between the

villagers and their traditional rivals, the neighbouring Hakkas, 'as a form of restricted warfare' (160) in which the rules are agreed upon by the village elders from both sides beforehand, and where he himself takes up the double role of 'linesman' and trainer. This Dickensian set-piece is one of the comic high points of the story. Once the game is set in motion, Wallace, who begins as 'discrete adviser' soon finds himself 'in the part of goggling spectator' (162) as the exuberance of the teams gives the game its own logic but also makes it entirely unpredictable. In this element of unpredictability, inscribed in the 'eccentric course' of the ball in the narrative (166–7), the bonds of traditional sociality are symbolically loosened, releasing Wallace from their grip. But it is precisely this unpredictability which suggests that Wallace's effort to nudge his community towards a reformed and more harmonious social order will dissipate. At the end of the match, all that the teams can do, with Wallace among them, is to stare at the ball, 'swerving, sliding, slipping, even … zig-zagging … in defiance of the laws of physics' till it disappears 'without trace – into the bamboos' (167). Though the feuding energies of the two villages are exhausted temporarily, 'the boundaries remained unchanged' (168).

The narrative returns, in the shortest and final part, to the family as the location where individual progress can make a more permanent difference. Mr Poon's illness and death follow in rapid succession; Ah Lung's disgrace leaves Wallace as the successor, and he moves into the position of patriarch with little effort, expanding the family's business interest and its fortune. 'At home there was more food'; Wallace's authority, 'diffidently worn', is obeyed without deference, and in the new regime, the rituals of old are replaced by festive celebrations both spontaneous and vital. Wallace's passage into 'Chinese' ethnicity seems complete, but the narrative adds a problematic coda to this assimilationist reading. At the very end of the novel, Wallace has a dream in which he feasts at a banquet where the main delicacy is the brains of a living monkey. The identities of the other guests are known but strangely unrecognisable, and Wallace sits at the head of the elaborately-laid table:

Ivory chopsticks and a long, curved spoon with sharp edges, such as might be used to excavate marrow-bones, lay before him, unsullied, on a silver cruet... From behind the wings of his chair a square box, covered by a black drape, was placed on the table. Although he had not noticed it before, there was an exquisite silver hammer in the centre of the banqueting board. It had a slim, flexible-looking horn handle. A pair of long, female hands, the nails enamelled, appeared out of the shadows and placed a tiny spirit lamp by the hammer. A miniature cauldron, slightly bigger than a thimble, hung above the flame from a glittering toy tripod. Wisps of almost colourless smoke rose from the drop of clear amber oil it contained.

The drape was pulled off the box to reveal it as a cage. Inside the cage, immobilised with manacles around its feet and hands, an iron band clamped around the top of its head, the dome of which protruded through a hole in the top, was a young monkey. It wrinkled bloodless lips back, baring its teeth in rage and terror. Its head had been shaved, leaving a tonsure in the centre of the skull. A knotted blue vein throbbed beneath the rubbery membrane of scalp. Seen from above, the part of the monkey's cranium poking through the cage looked like a brown egg in its cup.

There was an expectant rattle as the diners reached for chopsticks. The woman's hand took up the hammer; another, a man's, the pot of now seething oil. The hammerhead glittered as it hovered a fraction at the top of the swing. It came down in a silver blur.

Bone peeled away easily on skin, like shell attached to a tissue of crinkling albumen. The oil hissed, popping as it encountered a slimy surface.

Wallace awoke... Beside him May Ling swallowed in her sleep. He pulled a blanket over her and waited for the dawn. (214–15)

In the erupting nightmare of the unconscious, assimilation is refigured as consumption, and the barbaric underside of a 'Chinese' civility rises from its ancient and buried darkness to overwhelm its latest victim. Wallace is both participant and observer of the time-honoured rituals of the banquet; its orderly seating, with Wallace 'in the place of honour' and meticulous choice and layout of implements, speak of refinement and civilisation, or the habitual practice of generations. Wallace is an insider to this group, but the shadowy 'diners' whom he cannot see, and the disembodied 'pair of long, female hands' also suggest his isolation in what is a collective occasion. As the focus moves onto the monkey in the second paragraph, the menace of the previous paragraph turns into a palpable terror. There is no reference to Wallace the diner; it is assumed that he continues to narrate as an observer of his dream. But the focalisation of the narrative at one particular point suggests a third and horrifying perspective for him: 'It came down in a silver blur.' The sentence, narrated by the third person, also carries the possibility of the monkey's point of view as it looks upward at the descending instrument. The consequences of this barbaric act are immediate and visible, but are too horrible to contemplate any further; there is no other suggestion of Wallace-as-monkey, and immediately after, he 'awoke'.

On the level of consciousness, Wallace is at home in his acquired ethnicity as the domestic harmony which prevails between him and May Ling shows. In this state, the cultural identity between the Chinese and Macanese catches up with the biological identity as an objective reality noted in the novel's opening. But in the realm of the unconscious, Wallace's sub-jectivity is much more indeterminate, hybridising emic and etic points of view as both ethnic insider and distanced observer, together with the third position of the monkey, strange and different, who is reduced to a sub-human captive and is literally eaten alive. In this phantasma of deracination, the ending of the novel, as a critique of the assimilationist narrative, constructs the self-consuming artefact of ethnic hybridity.

The Monkey King focuses on the Chinese family *in situ* wrestling with change and modernity. That such change is embodied in a cultural outsider inaugurates a thematic pattern which is visible in all of Mo's novels, but if Wallace as a latter-day Monkey King suggests the periodical eruptions of the forces of change in Chinese culture, Mo is deeply ambivalent about the impact which unorthodox individuals might have on inherited institutions and structures. This does not mean a commitment to preserving what is ancestral, but a firm recognition of the power of tradition to compel submission from any single individual, deliberately or unconsciously. Agency, or the ability to make a difference, is, in Mo's novels, largely illusory, and some of his other characters and protagonists have the imagination to see in the clear light of day what in Wallace can only be accommodated in the unconscious. In *Sour Sweet*, Mo's second novel, it is the Chinese family in diaspora which has to contend with the problematic transition from past to present, from natal to adopted home. And in the gendered imagination of the first two novels, the reformist antics of the marginal, Wallace Nolasco, confront the immobile 'Chineseness' of Lily Chen in *Sour Sweet*.

The Chinese family in diaspora:
Sour Sweet

THE first reviewers of *Sour Sweet* focused on the lives of
Chinese people in Britain which the novel represents; for them,
as for many readers in Britain, the novel was a way into a world
or a parallel space which they vaguely knew existed but was as
alien as the distant colony of Hong Kong itself. Published in
1982, *Sour Sweet* travels back twenty years to the arrival and
subsequent adventures of the Chen family in London during the
1960s, and situates this family story in relation to both the
community of Chinatown in central London and to suburban
life on the edge of the metropolis.[1] The novel consists of thirty-
six chapters which fall into three parts: Chapters One to Ten
introduce the main characters, Chen, his wife Lily, their young
son Man Kee, and Lily's sister Mui, and narrate their origins and
immigrant way of life in the early days of arrival; Chapters
Eleven to Twenty-two show the growth of the family and its
adaptation to new life in Britain. The remaining fourteen chapters are concerned with the fragmentation and reconstitution of
the family, leading to the denouement of Chen's disappearance
and Mui's marriage and departure. Woven into this family
anthropology, and the history of its growth and location, is the
narrative of that sinister quasi-family organisation, the triads,
whose subterranean operation underwrites life and sociality in
traditional Chinatown. For all its visible autonomy, the Chen
family cannot escape being embroiled in the violent triad feuds,
and Chen, without the knowledge of his wife, becomes a victim.
This interlocking narrative is foregrounded in the first two

parts, which systematically alternate a chapter on the Chen family with one on the triads, an arrangement which also enables Mo to play with continuities and contrasts between the two as social organisations.

The narrative can be read as constituted of two overlapping discourses and I will discuss these in this chapter. Through representations of the Chens and the triads, the ethnic Chinese or *intra-cultural* discourse focuses on the family as the site of cultural tradition, identity formation and social relations. The second, *inter-cultural* discourse, raises questions about the contact and conflict between Chinese and British cultures. In making the family the paradigm of the intra-cultural discourse, Mo enlarges on the project in *The Monkey King* which has opened up fictional perspectives of looking at – and satirising – Chinese culture through the Chinese family. The two novels further resemble each other in that change within the family, and by extension in cultural tradition, is generated by the impact of the outside world. Wallace in *The Monkey King* embodies this external incursion, and *Sour Sweet* complicates the theme by the Chens' wholesale migration to an alien culture.

As we have seen in Chapter 1, contemporary theorising has put a premium on cultural identity as a 'process' rather than a *given*. To quote Stuart Hall again: 'Identity is not as transparent or unproblematic as we think. Perhaps instead of thinking of identity as an already accomplished fact, which the new cultural practices then represent, we should think, instead, of identity as a 'production' which is never complete, always in process, and always constituted within, not outside, representation.'[2] The realist novel may not be 'new', but it is certainly one of those 'cultural practices' which has established fiction as the site of identity production. As we have come to understand it, the realist novel, in the mimetic process which is its *raison d'être*, not only constitutes multiple identities, both individual and collective, but also puts into circulation the different vantages – or positions – from which identity as process can be inaugurated, determined and contested. Simultaneously, the realist novel hangs its narrative on the peregrinations, both internal and external, of its protagonists, constituting their psychological complexities and interlocutions of received social and cultural realities. Mo's comment, that the 'most fundamental task of the novelist [is] making people live on the page',[3] is true to the realist tradition even though it says little about the internal complexities and varieties that the tradition has developed through its distinguished practitioners or his own strategies which change from one novel to another.

Mo seems to have created in Lily Chen, its woman protagonist, a character fully formed from the early years of her life, whose passage through the novel unfolds as a series of dramatic demonstrations of what she is rather than what she is becoming. This is also what distinguishes Lily from Wallace; we know very little of Wallace's origins or his life before he becomes a member of the Poon family, and Wallace has no memory of the past to speak of. As a character, Lily's strong sense of herself is grounded on her unique upbringing which Mo describes in detail in the opening chapter, and which is invoked from time to time by the narrator and by Lily herself. One can read *The Monkey King* as a symbiosis of self- and family transformation enabled in large measure by the absence of a prior history, but Mo offers another vantage on character and destiny in *Sour Sweet* which is much more deterministic, in that it focuses on character as an irreducible core of beliefs and habits formed early in life, and which continues to manifest itself and define the passage through life regardless of external changes. If *The Monkey King* sees the past as a point of departure for Wallace, *Sour Sweet* narrates Lily's many returns to *her* past throughout the novel.

This shift in vantage on character is part of a different narrative and critique of the Chinese family in *Sour Sweet*. There are two related aspects to this difference: First, Wallace's marginality as outsider is replaced by Lily whose solid presence embodies the family's values and traditions. Lily's pre-eminence is possible largely because of the family's displacement to a foreign terrain, and thus the second, and crucial measure of difference in *Sour Sweet* is the diasporal pressures upon the

Chinese family as a minority social and cultural unit, charged with the duty of cultural preservation in an environment of majority ignorance and indifference. As Khachig Tölölian observed, 'Diaspora' signifies a 'semantic domain that includes words like immigrant, expatriate, refugee, guest-worker, exile community, overseas community, ethnic community... Diasporas are the exemplary communities of the trans-national moment.'[4] In *Sour Sweet*, the Chinese characters are diasporal in all of the meanings which Tölölian identifies; in its geographical dislocation, the 'Chineseness' which we have seen fictionalised in *The Monkey King* is transformed and reconfigured and, through this momentous shift, Mo installs another critique of Chinese culture which takes in his own experience of living as a cross-cultural subject in metropolitan London.

In *The Monkey King*, Wallace begins as an outsider. But right from the start of *Sour Sweet*, Mo shows, through Lily, and her sister Mui, what it can mean for an individual and specifically, a woman, to be subjected to the irresistible patriarchal moulding of an orthodox Chinese family. The sisters' identities are stamped by their father, and it is this determinism which makes *Sour Sweet* a much bleaker novel than *The Monkey King*, especially in the story of Lily and her resistance to the changes that geographical relocation inevitably brings to her own family in London. *The Monkey King* is about a family in evolution, *Sour Sweet* about a family where change, though inevitable, is stubbornly denied. However, Mo has not turned his back on comedy, and the novel relishes the effects of family determinism in Lily's strength of character and purpose in an alien environment as much as in her intransigence.

'Perhaps the difference in the two sisters' characters', observes the third-person narrator of *Sour Sweet*, 'was the product of upbringing rather than of any innate traits of the personality' (10); in Lily's case, her 'father's attitude may have encouraged the growth of the aggressive side' (10) of her character. A martial arts champion in his home province in southern China, Lily's father is badly defeated in a combat with practitioners from the north. This humiliating experience intensifies his desire to pass on his skills to his offspring as proof of their enduring worth. The child Lily has no choice but to submit to her father's special interpretation of family and cultural tradition, and from the age of five to ten, is subject to the punishing physical discipline demanded of a martial arts initiate. Her body is literally the bearer of this familial culture, and the novel frequently describes her trimness, and swift and graceful movements, in order to underline the process by which culture comes to appear as innate and 'natural'.

The notion of punitive self-discipline as character-forming also becomes for Lily a personal creed, as does the veneration of age and ancestors which her own submission to parental authority exemplifies. These guide her actions and relations within the family in later life, and form the most conscious and unshakeable tenets of her understanding of 'Chineseness', for herself and for her family. What was instilled in early life has, for Lily, become instinct and habit, and involves minimal self- and cultural reflexiveness. Typically circular in thinking, she knows she is 'Chinese' because she does things in the 'Chinese' way, and being 'Chinese' means being what she is and doing what she does. Through Lily, cultural identity is posited as the completed process of early life in the family; once formed, this identity is manifested through life, and the narrative shows the unfolding, rather than transformation or complication, of Lily as a 'Chinese' subject. Migration only serves to intensify this given identity, to reduce it, in Lily's consciousness, to its formative elements which then mass and coagulate to become a bulwark against change.

Most of the time, Lily's thoughts are inextricable from an overriding desire for continuity and cohesion within the family. She has few doubts about how she should behave as wife, mother, and younger sister to Mui, or about those roles which Chen, their son Man Kee, and Mui occupy and are duty-bound to perform. And mutuality is subject, as much as the self, to inherited family tradition and hierarchies of gender and age. I will turn to these hierarchies, which the novel also represents as trans-familial, later on in the chapter. The strength demanded of the self in martial arts training has its corollary in force inflicted upon an opponent during combat; Lily, in ordering the self, also develops a propensity for ordering others. This translates into an abrasiveness in her management of family relations, especially when she thinks she is frustrated and opposed by the others' dilatoriness, or that her notions of 'Chineseness' are somehow challenged by their behaviour. But it is against outsiders that the 'aggressive side' in her character is best demonstrated. The strict boundaries she draws between family and the world, inside and outside, differentiate absolutely what is 'Chinese' from what is not. Lily cannot observe or comment on British people and their behaviour without disapproval, as if they are potential or actual threats to her and her family which must be kept at bay, or are imagined opponents in a fight wherein she must win or lose all.

For Lily as a child, then as a married woman with her own family, one of the assumed principles of her own 'Chineseness' is the respect a woman owes to the man on whom she is dependent. Cultured in a strict patriarchal tradition, Lily is, however, not always its reliable bearer; her strong will works against the unproblematic transmission of her female submissiveness from paternal to marriage home, and the diasporal isolation of the Chens opens up opportunities in which she can assume control over both husband and family. In a light-hearted instance early in the novel, Mo shows Lily performing her duty as wife. Once again, food is the cultural currency of this exchange:

> Lily Chen always prepared an 'evening' snack for her husband to consume on his return at 1.15 a.m. This was not strictly necessary since Chen enjoyed at the unusually late hour of 11.45 p.m. what the boss boasted was the best employees' dinner in any restaurant... Lily still went ahead and prepared broth, golden-yellow with floating oily rings, and put it before her husband when he returned. She felt she would have been failing in her wifely duties otherwise. Dutifully, Chen drank the soup he raised to his mouth in the patterned porcelain spoon while Lily watched him closely from the sofa. It was far too rich for him... Four years ago, at the beginning of

their marriage, Chen had tried leaving just the last spoonful but Lily's reproachful eyes were intolerable. She was merciless now, watching him with sidelong glances from the sofa…

Chen would have liked a biscuit but Lily was unrelenting here as well. Sweet after salty was dangerous for the system, so she had been taught; it could upset the whole balance of the dualistic or female and male principles, *yin* and *yang*… For four years, therefore, Chen had been going to bed tortured with the last extremities of thirst but with his dualistic male and female principles in harmony. This was more than could be said for Lily, Chen often thought, who concealed a steely will behind her demure exterior. (2–3)

Here, as elsewhere in the novel, Lily is a model of the wife's servitude to the husband, rigid but unimpeachable. Comedy seeps from the play between Lily's punctilious adherence to her inherited gendered role and the transfer of power from Chen to her that the everyday soup ritual encodes. The more correct Lily is in being 'wife', the more Chen is intimidated; exercising her will but seemingly oblivious of her domination, she has got Chen where she wants him as he ruefully takes the measure of the woman he has married. Patriarchal hierarchy is preserved but also transgressed through the peculiar ritual invented by Lily in which Chen is a reluctant but docile partner. Her servitude is a tyranny.

One of the questions which *Sour Sweet* raises – and it is a question asked by other immigrant narratives – is how, and how much, an ancestral and natal culture is transmitted and transformed in the passage of diaspora. Through the Chens' marriage and home life, Mo represents continuity *in* disruption. In other words, Lily's 'Chineseness' is consciously sustained but, unconsciously and imperceptibly to herself, the positions and the perspectives which define this 'Chineseness' in the family have been reconfigured and re-engendered. The irony of this doubled perspective is made apparent in the persistent discrepancy between what Lily assumes and what the narrator makes visible. What 'Chineseness' is as it is reconstituted in Lily as woman subject and in London, looks much more indeterminate than her self-perception and self-identification would ever allow.

If we compare the soup ritual to the meals in the Poon family, and indeed, the relationship between the Chens to that of Wallace and May Ling, the difference is obvious. But the Chens' marriage is not actually presided over by a powerful patriarch like Mr Poon. Lily carries in herself the lineage of a patriarchal identity, but in the family's moving away from an ancestral home-place, the fault lines in this identity can emerge into the open in the first fractures of a 'Chinese' cultural inheritance. In its ambivalent relationship with a culture of origins, the diasporal journey – and narrative – is one of both alienation and liberation. Throughout *Sour Sweet*, Lily defers to Chen; he is never openly contradicted, and time and again, Lily has to restrain her impatient and active will to take into account his hesitations and phlegmatic disposition. But in all the important family decisions – moving out of London, starting their own take-away business, the education of Man Kee – it is Lily who takes the initiative, makes the plans and carries them through. She is not above subtle persuasion and manipulation – in the art of kung-fu, as she knows too well, guile can be indispensable in setting up the enemy for defeat. When she feels threatened closer to home, her interventions can become brutal as the fighter in her retaliates, as we can see in her open disagreement with Chen over the future of Man Kee. Contrary to her will to make Man Kee succeed in life, Chen quietly encourages his son's interest in gardening; father and son, watched by an increasingly jealous Lily, have been drawn into a wordless and intimate bond as they work the soil and grow plants in the garden. The full violence of Lily's reaction can be seen in the following extract:

> Lily stormed out of the room into the kitchen. That Husband should abet him [Man Kee] in his disobedience and wilfulness! She looked into the dark garden, her own eyes blurring and a lump forming in her throat. As bitter tears began to come, she opened the back door and strode down to the end of the garden, guided by the smell of the

compost-heap. She put her hands round Man Kee's mango plant and tugged at it. It would not come up. She bent her knees and pulled with her back as well as her arms. There was a subterranean tearing, the sound of small roots, tendrils, and delicate fibres shearing and snapping. Still it wouldn't come. Lily took a deep breath. She wiped cold sweat from her forehead. She strained, fighting the plant with her whole body. With louder vegetable groanings it began to come out of the earth. Another long pull and then the plant was uprooted with a single loud snap that seemed to come out of her own body, so that for a moment Lily wondered if she had cracked her own vertebrae. Her blood pounded in her ears; she was panting... She didn't very much care... She threw the plant on the compost heap and walked back up the garden slowly, the earth lumpy under the soles of her slippers. (255–6)

Lily's rage is palpable; passionate but cold, it translates into an act of destruction which is symbolic of her – matriarchal – uprooting of the organic bond between father and son. In doing so, as the passage also suggests, she runs the risk of causing herself serious injury, for as Chen's wife and Man Kee's mother and also the daughter of her own father, is her own identity not torn apart with this 'subterranean tearing' of the patriarchal bond? The violence of which Lily is capable in this wilful act does not make her a sympathetic character, but it does point to her tragic incapacity under patriarchy in that she cannot get what she wants without becoming victim to what she is, or in other words, what her culture has made her.

To Lily, Chen is husband, master, breadwinner and by virtue of the superiority which culture and necessity have conferred upon him, the only channel of her desires but also the main obstacle to them. But the narrator also shows how very often Lily has to negotiate within herself as to how to deal with this patriarchal double-bind, to square the circle, so to speak, of being 'a better man than her husband' and yet remain subordinate to him as the good 'Chinese' woman and wife. In this negotiation, she can appeal to received cultural beliefs, especially the need to balance *yin* and *yang*, the two terms denoting female and male cosmic forces in Taoist belief. We have seen this in the earlier soup ritual, and often this need for balance is what she invokes to justify her will over Chen – to compensate for his gender-guaranteed superiority over her. Lily is not in the least interested in the philosophical and spiritual underpinnings of this belief, but she pays it much more than lip-service for it has clearly structured her in profound and unconscious ways so that even though she does not reflect upon it, it is called up for contingent and habitual justification of her actions.

At the end of the novel, Lily is alone with Man Kee. The triads, who have liquidated Chen, continue to send cash remittances to Lily in a perverse logic of communal welfare. Pained at his absence, Lily wills herself to believe that he is still alive and has not abandoned his responsibility as husband. Gradually, to her surprise, she discovers that:

> she was content with what her life had become. She had loved, still loved Husband. She looked forward to the day he would return to her… But in the meantime how light-hearted she could feel! Surely Husband hadn't weighed on her like that? … it was as if a stone had been taken off her and she had sprung to what her height should have been. She thought she had found a balance of things for the first time, *yin* cancelling *yang*; discovered it not by going to the centre at once – which was a prude's way and untypical of her – but by veering to the extremes and then finding the still point of equilibrium. Man Kee was too young to understand this yet… But she could wait patiently for the day she could pass this knowledge, and other things, on to him.. She might have lost Husband for a while but she still had Son. Who could take him away from her? (278)

Chen's disappearance means that Lily is effectively a single mother – a very 'un-Chinese' family formation – although she would never dream of considering herself as such, and holds on tenaciously to the prospect of 'Husband's' return. But with father long gone, and now her husband as well, Lily emerges from being daughter and wife to becoming herself, 'sprung to what her height should have been'. In this phrase, the hidden metaphor of organic growth arrested and then resumed distantly echoes and counterbalances her own action of uprooting the plant in the garden – as if to suggest causally that her sense of liberation is consequent upon the earlier violence against the patriarchal bond which is also an act of self-destruction. Reading in this way, Lily is transformed from being a victim of external circumstances over which she has no control to becoming an agent in her self-transformation. The new self continues to define itself within the old terms: wife/husband, mother/son, *yin* and *yang*, but they no longer mean the same relationally. From being an external, dualistic other, *yang*, the male force, has first been 'cancelled', and then relocated within Lily herself and the matriarchal inheritance she will leave to her son. It is as if Lily is still seeing herself and reality through a 'Chinese' screen, but she has recomposed the images on the screen so that they now bear the unmistakable imprint of her identity. The ending is poignant, full of both promise and foreboding, especially for Man Kee.[5]

Lily is characterised by disciplinarian and violent tendencies, and is riddled with cultural myopia and prejudices. But for all that, she is a very attractive and engaging character, active, vigorous, animated by a powerful will that refuses to allow the hardships of her situation as a new immigrant to become obstacles to her desires. Unsparing of her shortcomings, the narrative also devotes considerable space to her practical ingenuity, her entrepreneurial spirit, and later, her fortitude under distress. Stoical endurance never devolves into timidity for Lily while her insensitivity and habitual brusqueness, which at times alienate both her husband and sister, are tempered by displays of concern and affection that testify to an unshakeable belief in the superior demands of family and kinship over self. Fascinating in herself, Lily is the veritable source of the drama and good humour of *Sour Sweet*; she is the most outstanding woman character in Mo's novels, the internal archetype to which most of the minor women characters in Mo's novels refer.

Unlike Lily, Mui is spared her father's training, and left to cultivate what are perceived as the more feminine arts – cooking and flower arranging – in 'Chinese' culture, and the novel shows in a minor key how paternal neglect has invested her with the flexibility and adaptability that will enable her ultimate transformation. Quietly and imperceptibly, she grows out of Lily's shadow and develops and deploys the skills of crossing between family and world which her sister can never really fathom. We see her as a new arrival transfixed by *Crossroads* and *Coronation Street*, and how these soap operas help to induct her into 'British' society, and enable her to acquire the basic English idioms of social exchange. Mui has a curiosity about the 'ordinary' people represented in these programmes, and her riveted attention as their lives unravel before her on television every day silently defies Lily's hostile indifference. Though confined within the Chen family, Mui has begun to recognise and identify with the outside world, and this is gradually translated into actual friendships with neighbours and the drivers – the 'aitchgevees' – who patronise the Chens' take-away. While Lily takes control of the front-counter, and dominates the narrative foreground, from time to time Mui emerges – literally – from the unnarrated backroom space of the take-away to offer solutions to the problems arising from Lily's stubborn ignorance of the world around her. She arranges Lily's driving lesson with an 'aitchgevee', and Chen's father's trip to England, and deals with tax demand notes and visiting social welfare inspectors. In these forays of Mui's, the reader is given a periodic measure of her growing difference from Lily until the time comes near the end of the novel when, contrary to Lily's wish, she moves out to start a family of her own. The story of the two sisters speaks of the organic evolution of the single-cell family in the alien diasporal environment, its division into separate but related units within an apparently uniform immigrant mass. What we also witness is a cultural evolution within the immigrant community which has ramifications for the society beyond it. As an emergent and more forward-looking immigrant woman subject,[6] Mui's own home, one can imagine, will be liberated from most of the racial and cultural prejudices which characterise Lily's, and this in turn points towards the relocated

'Chinese' family as the site of cross-cultural contacts and negotiations rather than as the closed – and enclosed – space of
ancestral heritage. Mui's daughter is Anglo-Chinese, the offspring of her liaison with an 'aitchgevee' which the narrative,
through Mui herself, hints at but offers no details about. The
cultural symbolism of the child's racial hybridity – both within
and without the Chinese community – is palpable.

But the characterisation and narrative of Mui are both problematic. First of all, the aligning of the 'feminine' in 'Chinese'
culture with skills of negotiation and mediation replicates a
well-rehearsed gender stereotype. More importantly, there are
few details as to how Mui *becomes* this difference: since her
progress is given considerably less narrative space than Lily's
intransigence, it appears both marginal and mysterious. This is
obviously a formal artistic strategy of Mo's choosing, and *Sour
Sweet* rehearses the pattern set up in *The Monkey King* in which
narrative hangs largely on the fortunes of the protagonist. But it
does mean that the representation of the immigrant 'Chinese'
family is dominated by the focus upon a singular woman subject
who entrenches the boundaries between her ancestral and
adopted 'homes'. The reader is forced to share, at least in part,
Lily's blindness about her own sister, and though aware of the
promise which Mui's subjectivity holds, we are left unsure of
the ground on which it is constituted. Mui's history is incom-
plete, and this needs to be taken into account especially since the
novel was (and may still be) read as a cultural guide to the Chinese
community in Britain in a situation where texts – fictional or
otherwise – produced by and about the community remain few
and far between.[7] In 1982, when *Sour Sweet* was first published,
the characterisation of Mui offered a glimpse of new subject
formations within the Chinese community largely invisible to
the majority British view. Ironically, in marginalising Mui,
Sour Sweet also becomes part of a textual history in which
subjects like her continue to be displaced from greater public
recognition.[8]

Mui is not the only character to grow away from Lily's
'Chineseness' in the evolutions of the diasporal Chinese family.

The novel looks further ahead in representing the relationship between Lily and her son, Man Kee, and here the mother's determination to shape her son within a single tradition, and thus perpetuate her cultural heritage, comes up most sharply against the equally irresistible acculturation of the son into 'British' society in the process of education outside the family. Jealous of Man Kee's time away at school, Lily is even more discomforted by the trickle of information he gives her about a world from which she is excluded by the language barrier and her own cultural prejudices, a world which she can hardly understand, and which clearly does not measure up to her strict notions of education as discipline. As she senses her son moving away from her well-defined orbit into what she considers an alien and reprobate culture, Lily is first baffled and then alarmed, and decides immediately to send him to extra lessons in the school in Chinatown. This and other remedies, like teaching Man Kee kung-fu so that he can retaliate against the bullies in the school playground, only serve to make his life more difficult, though, still young, he has yet to experience the cultural tensions in his situation as personal conflict. In Man Kee, Mo gives a history – and an identity formation – to another diasporal 'Chinese' subject emerging from the ancestral womb of the family. The story of Man Kee has just begun, but already it is the site of an inter-generational dialectic: between maternal will and the son's autonomy, between an ancestral past, imagined and made known, and an unknown present and future, between ethnic retrenchment within the family and a multicultural dynamic that is becoming institutionalised in society at large. How this dialectic would work itself out was, in 1982, a question which *Sour Sweet* raised but did not, or could not, really address.

Besides the Chens, the novel is populated by minor China-town characters: the staff in the restaurant where Chen used to work; Mr Lo, Chen's colleague who eventually marries Mui; and Mrs Law, a rich older woman whom the sisters first meet in a supermarket and who then becomes a family friend, offering Mui shelter before the birth of her illegitimate daughter. Two points are of interest here: the symbiotic extension of kinship into communal bonds as the family reaches out laterally to seek its own kind, and the absence of class barriers, or rather the way ethnic identification overrides class differences in the family's location in community, as is clearly evident in the sisters' meeting and friendship with the genteel Mrs Law, and the latter's courteous relationship with Mr Lo. Again, ritual is the key, both the linguistic rituals which facilitate the sisters' approach to Mrs Law and which continue despite their growing intimacy, and the touching etiquette of behaviour which enables Mrs Law and Mr Lo to observe gender boundaries but still express concern for each other. The channelling of reciprocity through ritual represents one of the novel's most positive perspectives on 'Chinese' culture, and the scenes it informs are animated by the characters' comic awkwardness as they spontaneously negotiate received social conventions with strangers and acquaintances.

In its representations of the family in community, the novel, however, focuses on a much more sinister set of ritualistic practices and the culture of violence it encodes but also seeks to legitimate. In the first part of the novel, Mo devotes as much narrative attention to the triad organisation in Chinatown as to the Chens. In a number of scenes in this part, we see the triad's initiation ceremonies where new recruits mimic in ritual the heroic patriotism of the organisation's founders in the Qing dynasty, and are given rudimentary training in the martial arts by the current leader and enforcer, Red Cudgel. Cohesion is justified and mystified in a mythical origin and an invented tradition, and forged by strict discipline with infractions punished, without fail, by violence. The hierarchies of age and gender that define the triad's internal structure are remarkably like those we have seen in the Chen family, and its collective identity is predicated on a narrative of ancestral origins which is no less shaded, embellished, and subject to selective emphasis as Lily's remembered 'Chineseness'. Collective survival, however, is a matter of organisation and business acumen, and the triad leaders' meetings about policy are in the same spirit as Lily's determination to cajole and rally her family to her idea of their own take-away. As family units, the triads and the Chens under

Lily enact the discourse of orthodoxy in the narrative of 'Chinese-ness'. But at the same time, the fault lines of geographical dislocation and generational differences which are common to both open up the critique of 'Chinese' orthodoxy in the text.

In the scenes of triad violence, Mo puts into practice what he has learned about fighting and writing about fights. This violence, glimpsed in the earlier passage on Lily's act of destruction, is extreme and graphic, and the fight scenes are fashioned in excruciating, blow-by-blow detail; Mo has honed his craft well, and there is a sense that he relishes the challenge in making verbal language perform the kind of cinematic realism popularised by Hong Kong kung-fu films. It is possible, however, to extrapolate a point of value from this emphasis on detail, for it shows how violence which might begin as punitive rapidly degenerates into an end in itself, and in doing so, demonstrates the moral bankruptcy of the triad, completely undermining its claims to be the guardians of the welfare and good order of their own kind.[9] In rhetoric, the triad is unremittingly chauvinist and racist against outsiders – the rest of white British society – but all its violent energies are channelled inwards in internecine feuds among the leaders or against hapless working men like Chen. It is hard to tell whether, besides their own survival and aggrandisement, the triads ultimately differentiate between inside and outside.

The alienating violence of the fight scenes and the plight of Chen as victim of the triads are the two wings of Mo's critique of the triads as an orthodox 'Chinese' institution. For the triads too are a sort of family that has emigrated to foreign soil. Mo himself says: 'That's what [*Sour Sweet*] was trying to do – to show how close the Chen family are to the criminals. What makes these criminal societies possible are the same values that Chinese people like to espouse. Respect for elders, the tradition of self-help which leads to a distrust of the state…, the fact that the family is the unit of survival, not the individual.'[10] But from another vantage, it could be argued that what we see in the triads is nothing less than family values running amok, in a diasporal situation in which the family operates in a social vacuum.

Despite their move to London, none of the Chinese characters, except for Mui, recognises, understands, or claims access to British social and legal institutions. For them, the metropolis is the site of labour, not of citizenship; secluded within their own ethnic group, they turn to each other for their affective needs, and in times of crisis, to the triads for help and succour. In the triads, the economic motive of the immigrant worker – or his desire for a better life for himself and his family – is distorted as unrestrained greed; kinship and ethnic bonds are recast as the chains of exploitation; veneration for ancestors and the old becomes the justification for oppression, discipline, coercion and the threat of death. Mrs Thatcher once famously – or infamously – declared: 'There is no such thing as society; there are only individuals and their families.' Where 'society' as a community and a site of co-operation is absent or unrecognised, the triads fill the vacuum and become the only 'society'; what *Sour Sweet* shows is the tragedy and terror that individuals and families can suffer when this takes place. At the same time, it also diagnoses the interactions of 'Chinese' myopia and prejudices and 'British' neglect which allowed the triad sub-culture to flourish, a law unto itself.

I have said earlier on that Lily cannot look upon British life and people outside the family without feeling a sense of repugnance. In the novel, 'Britain' or 'London' is under-narrated; it is the imaginary other, the function of Lily's remembered and transplanted 'Chineseness', and her sense of threat and encirclement. When it does appear, 'Britain' is mediated by the alienated Chinese characters, or embodied in state functionaries – tax inspectors, welfare officers – who are stereotyped by their roles and seen through suspicious immigrant eyes. But if the 'Chinese' characters care little about 'Britain', 'Britain' is also prepared to leave them alone most of the time. Discursively, 'Britain', as a host culture, enters into the picture, for Lily performs one kind of immigrant subjectivity for whom assimilation is never an option, and contact means contamination. Lily's immigrant subjectivity is ill-disposed to cope with the changing realities of life in Britain, and strenuously resists movements towards a new subjectivity, unlike Mui's or Man Kee's, which crosses family and society, and can fuse, at least on a quotidian level, 'Chinese' and 'British' practices.

But Mo is not interested in fashioning Lily as a victim of British racial and cultural prejudices, or as the disoriented migrant from the colonies – which we see, for example, in the novels of Sam Selvon. The Chens' 'Britain', for one thing, is scarcely monolithic: their most loyal customers are the continentally nomadic HGV drivers, and the English man they know best bears the name of Constantinides. It would also be overstating the case to align Lily with the marginals, valorised in certain versions of postcolonial theory, who challenge imperial or metropolitan oppression, or actively resist assimilation into a dominant culture.[11] What the novel does is to relocate 'Britain' as an immigrant discourse poised at the moment of transition, which is also a point of contestation and rupture, in which mono-ethnic and monocultural norms nonetheless bear traces of a hybrid *beyond* struggling to be named. 'Britain' in *Sour Sweet* can be seen as a fictional telescope through which changing formations in identity and subjectivity are brought close to home to a reading public, to enable, in turn, their visual and perceptual, cognitive and empathetic reconsiderations of their own locations.

Equally reductive would be to read the novel as simply the private history of an immigrant family though this is what the film adaptation, *Soursweet*, focuses on – the scriptwriter, Ian McEwan, suggesting 'that the film's real subject was Lily and Chen, the marriage, their relationship, their adventure in coming to England, the clash of their different personalities'.[12] The simplifying constraints of translating from one medium to another, which McEwan interestingly discusses, led to his decision to lay the emphasis there so that in the film,[13] the significant cross-references between family and triad have all but disappeared. In focusing on the family, McEwan and Newell also decided, for cost-saving reasons, to shift the time-frame from the 1960s to the 1980s.[14] This is much more problematic. As I pointed out earlier on, the novel raises a number of questions about the generation of immigrants in the early 1960s, like the Chens, from the vantage point of 1982, questions which, however, could not be further pursued until more recently. The film's strategy simply obliterates the identity differences between an earlier generation of immigrants and more recent arrivals or, indeed, British-born Chinese.[15] In making the Chens not only paradigmatic but also trans-historical, the film frames the 'Chinese' community much more uniformly than it actually is or has been. *Sour Sweet* has its significant place in Mo's *œuvre* and the geography of contemporary British literature and culture; McEwan's *Soursweet*, which begins within this compass, also disorients it. That this is so is inscribed in the anecdote of how McEwan took Timothy Mo to see the set of the film, and praised the scene in which Mui translated for Chen's father in front of the coffin. The scriptwriter 'was astonished' when he discovered that he was really complimenting himself; the author had never written the scene in the way it was filmed.[16] Mo's response to this discovery remains unrecorded.

History from the margins:
An Insular Possession[1]

AN *Insular Possession* represents a deliberate turning away from the domestic chronicles of *The Monkey King* and *Sour Sweet*. In his third novel, and also in the fourth, *The Redundancy of Courage*, Mo's imaginative range reaches out to two separate crisis locations in Asia where historical and political upheavals changed the courses of nations and communities. The subject matter of *An Insular Possession*, the Sino-British conflict that led to the Opium War and the establishment of Hong Kong as a colony and city port in the Far East in the nineteenth century, is epical in scope, and resonates of Virgil's epic on the founding of Rome. As realist fiction, it is a successor to nineteenth-century novels set against the broad canvas of European wars such as *Vanity Fair* or *War and Peace*, but also intervenes in the tradition with its remembering of Europe's long neglected Chinese frontier. In the geographical movement away from Europe and its own late twentieth-century moment, the novel, as a project of memory, puts a further postcolonial spin on its venerable realist inheritance. This rich and complex literary undertow surges beneath the opening description of the Pearl River as it enters the delta region centred on the pre-eminent trading port of southern China, Canton:

> The river succours and impedes native and foreigner alike; it limits and it enables, it isolates and it joins. It is the highway of commerce and it is a danger and a nuisance. Children fall off native craft; drunken sailors topple from the decks of the Company's chequered ships. Along with

the rest of the city's effluvia the river sweeps the victims out to sea... At its mouth it stains the clear blue sea yellow-brown, the colour of tea as drunk in London... Where the river rises thousands of miles inland it seems already pregnant – with silt, with life, and with the opposite of life. (1)

This description specifically situates *An Insular Possession* in the compass of narratives like Dickens's *Our Mutual Friend* and Conrad's *Almayer's Folly*, both beginning with rivers – one in England, the other in Borneo – and Eliot's *The Mill on the Floss*, where the river functions as a kind of discursive nexus. In Mo's novel, the Pearl River is at once the geographical site of imperial conflict, the spatial and temporal figuration of imperialism's changing fortunes, and the naturalising trope of its processes.[2]

Mo had once declared, 'I hate the historical novel... There's an inherent bathos about the form of the historical novel – people put modern language into these characters' mouths... I like the historical novel as written by someone like Peter Ackroyd because ... he uses the old language'[3] *An Insular Possession* is written in the present tense, and in the reconstructed idiom of the nineteenth-century novel. This idiom is imprinted, as we can see, in the opening paragraph and throughout the narrative, not only in descriptive moments but also in the dialogue of the characters. But it is the fear and loathing of the bathetic, rather than a conscious striving towards some kind of historical authenticity, which prompts Mo to imagine and create an idiom of the past. This point is augmented in his admission that he liked 'the idea that everybody's notion of the Opium Wars in sixty years' time will be *mine*'. He continued:

You see, our version of 19th-century London is not really Mayhew's or Karl Marx's, it's Dickens's version, which is a complete falsification... I've tried to make the economic analysis of it truthful, and sincere. I may have done violence to the facts at some stage, but you can rely on it as a *sincere* representation of that time and place.[4]

Necessarily perspectival, historical fiction also necessarily lies; Mo deliberately blurs the boundaries between fact and the factitious and in doing so, raises serious questions about authenticity as a criterion of value for historial fiction. Within its postcolonial frames, this cross-boundary awareness signals the novel's radical undertaking in its implicit critique of the discourse of history-writing traditionally premised on 'object-ivity' and claims to truth. In announcing that what he offers is his own 'version' of the past, and in wanting it to become *the* decisive reading, Mo acknowledges the innate subjectivity of his novel. At the same time, he is also arguing for the power of fiction, much more than conventional histories, to intervene in shaping our collective memory and understanding of the past. In this chapter, I will explore those strategies of narrative in *An Insular Possession* which perform fiction's critique of history-writing, and which enable Mo to be both subjective and 'sincere' at the same time.[5]

In the novel, which is Mo's late twentieth-century take on the historical epic, the formal and cross-boundary inventiveness co-exists uneasily with a thematic argument for ethnic and cultural segregation that we have already seen in *Sour Sweet*. Mo's earlier narrative of Chinese immigrants in London actually shows how Chinese and British cultures are kept discrete, fenced in their separate worlds, and this segregation is driven home not only by the dominant focus on Lily, but also the minimal attention to the British location. In a deliberate reversal, *An Insular Possession*, though set in Canton and Hong Kong, focuses almost exclusively on expatriates and colonials, and averts its gaze from most of what can be called 'native', that is to say, Chinese characters, scenes, customs, social relations. It is as if the novel has crossed cultures in order to assert incommensur-ability as paradigm in our understanding of cultural relations. Some justification for this can be derived from the subject matter of *An Insular Possession*: after all, it is a narrative of war, of a contest between two empires grounded not only on the material interests of trade and power, but on cultural differences which could not be overcome or finessed by diplomacy. On the other hand, it could equally be argued that the choice of the Opium War as subject matter demonstrates, once again, the persistent logic of cultures in irreconcilable conflict which shapes Mo's novels. Long before the crisis of war, this logic has worked its way into the narrative, to shape the optic of the third-person narrator as he dwells on the barriers between expatriate and native:

> Aunt Remington is pretending to read under a parasol in the bright sunshine of the lawn's centre; actually she is … enjoying the fragrance of the exotic blooms. Very few are familiar to her and the tiny, old Chinese gardener has no English at all, not even the names of his gorgeous charges. '*Lairng fa*,' he says grinning and pointing at the flowers, then, under Aunt's insistent interruption, '*Lairng fa*,' he exclaims again, of quite a different species. He really is an aggravating old fellow, Aunt thinks crossly. They inherited him, of course. He and his beautiful growths were there long before they ever came and will be long after they have departed. To the old gardener, the present occupiers are of less significance than the blooms of a single season, which may fade and die, but then return the following year, which is more than the tenants of the house ever do. He sees himself, with some justification, as the garden's real owner. (93–4, italics in original)

Here, the expatriate woman, Mrs Remington, is guided by a native informant in the first stage of an imperial passage: the naming, cataloguing, and inventory of the local flora and fauna, or what is 'natural', and therefore most irreducibly 'native', to the prospective colony.[6] She is being implicitly inducted into a particular history of cultural exchange, one narrated in terms of native reception and western receptivity, for the lesson she is given is one which the gardener, as an old retainer, has presumably given before to her predecessors, and is keen to repeat with this latest arrival on the local landscape. It is a familiar cross-purpose. The would-be ethnographer elicits nomenclature, the native informant obliges with description – '*lairng fa*': nice flower. Mrs Remington not only signally fails to learn but in her very irritability, shows a resistance to this history she has inherited. From now onwards, history, as a narrative of cross-cultural contact, has to be rewritten as two discrete histories, each enclosed within itself, unable to articulate itself to the other. Again, we have seen a version of this rewritten narrative in Lily in *Sour Sweet*, who carries 'China' in her head as an imaginary geography superimposed on her British habitat. The process of rewriting is renewed, early in *An Insular Possession*, in the gardener's inability to vary his speech or make himself understood; the speaking native or subaltern has no place in the novel as it unravels as the narrative of nineteenth-century young expatriates and, very occasionally, their women companions in the garden of adventure which is Canton and China. The encounter between the gardener and Mrs Remington enacts an instance of the dynamic of incommensurability that runs through the novel and cuts across another of its vital interests – that of marginality.

Consistent with Mo's interest in marginal characters which we have already seen in the first two novels, the American nationality of the two protagonists of *An Insular Possession* – Gideon Chase and Walter Eastman – places them as outsiders to the Sino-British conflict, and suggests history written from the vantage-point of the disempowered third party. The scenes of conflict are refracted through their observations, and a central theme of the novel concerns their struggle to make their dissenting voices heard in the expatriate community dominated by the British traders. Thus *An Insular Possession* is history seen by and through the experience of outsiders who try to transform themselves into social actors, and in the process, open up a space of engagement between the west and China which counters the hegemony of mercantilist interests, desires and practice. In this respect, the novel implicitly positions itself as the fictional alternative to both imperial (British) and nativist (Chinese) versions of history, and confronts history and identity as constituted of voices whose possibility has not been previously imagined. That these voices are invested with an American nationality clearly suggests that Mo has taken into account the ambivalent position of the United States during the period of the novel; an ex-colony hostile towards European expansionism, it is, however, as much interested in trade in China as the European imperialist nations.[7] But the release of these voices, hitherto unheard, marks the novel as late twentieth century, as contemporary.

As it writes the history of the period, this third-party narrative also installs a critique of the methods, procedures and ideological alignments of traditional historiography. *An Insular Possession* is a historical novel that is also metahistorical in that it parodies the lack of self-reflexiveness of much traditional historiography. In a number of essays published in the 1970s and 1980s, Hayden White has drawn attention to history as a fabrication that employs the strategies of creative literature and whose claims to factual truth and objectivity are always open to question.[8] More recently, Linda Hutcheon argues that contemporary historiographic metafiction raises the same issues about the relation between literary and historical discourses earlier theorised by White. *An Insular Possession* participates implicitly in the critique of those truth-bearing claims of traditional history-writing that prompt White's and Hutcheon's inquiries. It could be read as a fictional demonstration of how historical 'fact' is created out of the experiential 'event' by different narrative and rhetorical strategies. And by counterpointing these strategies throughout the text, Mo's novel further constructs the context of ideological forces at work to shape the history of the period.

History, as it is told in *An Insular Possession*, is not written in the form of a master narrative, or from the point of view of a single authority. Instead, it is a jumble of narratives, told by a multiplicity of voices, all jostling each other for supremacy. Furthermore, it could be said that *the devices* – the objective journalistic report, realistic visual representation, firsthand or eyewitness accounts – in which master narratives are often justified are counterpointed in the text, and each revealed, in turn, as inherently flawed. Foremost among these devices is the 'factual' report of the type seen in newspapers and journals on which traditional historiography has often relied upon for veracity. Much of the narrative of *An Insular Possession* is taken up by editions of the two journalistic publications, *Canton Monitor* and *Lin Tin Bulletin and River Bee,* arranged successively in the text and often reporting contrary versions of similar events. Through their juxtaposition, the novel implicitly asks: What is the 'truth' of an event? How can it be verified? Can it be verified?

The *Canton Monitor,* the voice and very often the propaganda of belligerent British commercial and imperial interests, is the establishment paper of the Pearl River Delta. Attacking all that stands in the way of British trade and, specifically, the traffic in opium, to the point of openly castigating Captain Charles Elliot, the commander of the British fleet, for being 'soft' on the Chinese, the *Canton Monitor* is history seen on a daily basis from the point of view of the colonialist supremacist. Against its version of 'facts', Chase's and Eastman's *Lin Tin Bulletin* resists with sympathetic reports on Elliot's activities and features on Chinese rituals, customs and literary culture. It tells of a world outside the expatriate cloister of trade and tiffin, club and cricket, and of a history that takes place elsewhere, to which its editors, Chase and Eastman, claim greater freedom of access and knowledge by virtue of their alibi as exiles from their own race and ethnic community. The narrative of *An Insular Possession* itself encloses the contest between two competing versions of history narrated by the newspapers. In doing so, Mo underlines the conflicting ideologies that inform them – the *Canton Monitor* asserting its hegemony and the *Lin Tin Bulletin* seeking to insert itself into the public discourse of the time by transgressing established boundaries of what can or cannot be known, and by fashioning itself as alternative.

Through the two newspapers, the novel also raises questions about what New Historicists have called 'the textuality of history'.[9] Newspaper reports are frequently regarded by historians as primary documents and indispensable in the verification of 'facts'. But the entire relation between such documents and historical truth is probed and satirised by the novel. The two newspapers in *An Insular Possession* are clearly shown to be embedded in the socio-cultural and ideological situation of those who produce them and to put strikingly different constructions on events. The self-fashioning of Chase and Eastman, through the medium of their newspaper, as idiosyncratic outsiders and fearless challengers to the British establishment further thickens the textual (and ideological) mediation of their reporting. In casting a critical eye on contemporary records of events as post factum constructions, Mo implicitly undermines the traditional historiographic practice of asserting the truth of 'what happened' on the basis of a study of extant 'sources'.

The novel also scrutinises other devices of recording the past and emphasises their questionable relations with truth. Besides the two protagonists, one of the prominent characters is the Irish painter O'Rourke, an old China-hand, well known for his painting of local scenes and events, who makes his living doing portraits of the wives of the merchants and traders. Very early on in the novel, O'Rourke corrects a drawing by Eastman of the Praia Grande at Macao, and adds the following caution: 'at your stage you might well be better advised *to copy from the work of a master, than to draw it from the life!*' (11, emphasis in original). The painter novice may well progress from being twice removed from reality, but the gap between his imagistic record and 'the life' is one built into the artistry or painting or drawing itself and is unbridgeable by even the most seasoned master.

Painting shades, highlights and conceals as much as it reveals; such aestheticising strategies are what constitute the painter's style. The kind of painting that O'Rourke does pulls in one direction towards an aesthetic mimesis, and in another towards a historical discourse – a discourse that is itself double, as it addresses both its manifest subject (scene, event, or person) and the latent subjectivity of the painter himself. This bifurcated movement enforces a relationship between painting as historiographic record and 'life' that is always mediated, ambivalent, and open to interpretation, distortion and falsification. It is significant that at the end of the novel, most of O'Rourke's paintings are supposed to be destroyed in a fire; what is left behind are only 'a sketch for a theatre programme' and, more pointedly, 'two early Daguerreotype photographs by an unknown hand' of two of his paintings. These 'do not inspire the conventional veneration which contemporaries appear to have felt' (582). The judgement of O'Rourke's work illuminates the fact that it is the subjectivity, or style, of the painter that is of historical interest and not the paintings themselves as historical records.

It is of course ironical that a remnant of O'Rourke's work should be preserved by the very medium, the 'Daguerreotype photographs', that has displaced it as historical record. O'Rourke himself correctly perceives that the photograph is the greatest threat and challenge to his continued monopoly of 'life representation', and his role as the visual historian of the Delta and its expatriate establishment. Chase and Eastman, in articles in the *Lin Tin Bulletin* promoting the new technology of the photoheliograph, show an awareness of its constructed nature which makes it akin to the strategies of the painter that it is about to displace:

> No two individual operators will ever take the same scene or portrait in quite the same fashion. We do acknowledge this. The minutest deviation in angle... framing... and moment selected to make the exposure ... – all or severally each contribute to the final result. It is quite surprising how tiny and apparently insignificant differences will be productive of hugely distinctive results... (523)

At the same time, they contextualise the new medium by seeing it as a site of negotiation between the contending political forces in which they themselves are situated:

> The heliographic method is at once *Democratic* and *Imperial*. Democratic because after a little simple trial and error, not to be compared with the labour of learning the painterly craft, excellent results may be secured by all. Imperial because it is a most voracious medium, which is capable of annexing the entire solid world and recreating it in two dimensions, instead of three. (523, emphasis in original)

Chase and Eastman seem to have grasped much of the significant, and paradoxical, import of this new technology: its elimination of artistic labour and judgement while enabling artifice and the production of the artificial. Both liberating and reductive, the photo becomes the natural medium for the two of them, and people and journalists like them, who are trying to operate between the 'Democratic' and 'Imperial'. Eastman exploits the potential of the photograph as manufactured – and artificial – record, and how this record can, in turn, guarantee their own evolving identities, from outsiders to alternative voices challenging the British enterprise. In the midst of a devastating British naval bombardment of the Chinese forts on the Pearl River, Eastman, with Chase as a silent witness, arranges a photograph to be taken of a dead Chinese soldier:

> Eastman and Wheeldon have a dead Chinese artilleryman between them, his bare powder-blackened arms around their necks, feet trailing on the ground – Eastman, who, Gideon notices, has not even the grace to give a guilty start. They drape the corpse over the breech of the cannon. Walter spots the rammer and his eyes brighten. He puts it into the dead man's hand, but it falls out. And again...
>
> Wheeldon tries to break the stick across his knee and fails, but, standing it against the cannon, he uses his sword to hack it in half. He strews the pieces at the dead gunner's feet.
>
> Walter kicks at a ruptured sand-bag to bring more debris down. Pulling at some wicker baskets filled with earth, he completes the scene of destruction. Wheeldon brings a tasselled lance from where it has been flung down by escaping soldiers, another pleasant touch. Walter now addresses himself to the management of the camera, he, Wheeldon, and it the only standing whole objects in the devastation. (442–3)

History is made as the fighting goes on, and is remade by Eastman, eyewitness, photographer and artistic director. The photograph duly appears in the *Lin Tin Bulletin* and confirms the *Bulletin* as friend to the Chinese and the conscientious objector to British military aggression. But the production of the photograph testifies to ideological manipulation that begs the question of the *Bulletin*'s difference from its imperial competitor, the *Canton Monitor*. In this respect, the critique of the devices of traditional historiography goes beyond the apparent juxtaposition of the decline of such devices and the ascendance of new technological media to unfathom a continuous – and ideologically driven – dynamic between them. *An Insular Possession* has its eye critically trained on diachronic processes that are not only germane to the period it narrates but also to its own late twentieth-century moment of rapidly expanding information technology.

In showing the manipulativeness of Eastman's actions, Mo casts implicit doubt upon the necessary moral righteousness of his character's counter-establishment position. This ambivalence is amplified, and re-embodied in a different way, in the narrative of Chase who is, in many ways, the more interesting and complex character. In the novel, Chase increasingly departs from Eastman, and follows another route in his own participation in history and history-making. Against prohibitions from both native and expatriate communities, Chase learns and acquires expertise in the Chinese language. If O'Rourke's and Eastman's domain is that of the visual, Chase, who serves as Captain Elliot's interpreter and translator, opens up the individual's negotiations with the verbal and discursive systems that are contending for domination over him and history. Scholarly and thoughtful, he is far more aware than the others of the imperative of truth, the difficulty of achieving it, and the implications of failure. To his first effort at rendering into English the letter from the Chinese Commissioner, Keshen, to Elliot, he adds: 'A true translation' (413). But clearly dissatisfied with this, he includes a postscript in which he re-reads the letter for its subliminal messages:

> N.B. This letter is unsatisfactory in the extreme. As well as employing the objectionable term Barbarian Eye for the Plenipotentiary [Elliot] and the offensive term *pin* for his ultimatum, neither of which characterised the mode of communication as between equals … the author of this most evasive message clearly means to indicate that he proposes a resumption of the Canton trade on the old terms and within the old system… The reference to the line of battle ships and the welfare of their crews

> represents a desire to indicate a consciousness of the
> possible weaknesses of the British expedition... The part-
> ing good wish with which his communication concludes is
> a barely disguised insult, which represents an attempt to
> degrade the Plenipotentiary and Superintendent of Trade
> to the status of a merchant and speculator. (413)

As translator, Chase attacks the opacity of Chinese official rhetoric and strives to reinstate a certain transparency of meaning to the language. In a reversal of the situation, he warns General Gough, the commander of the British fleet and Elliot's more belligerent replacement, that a proclamation he has to translate inviting the Chinese villages to surrender 'requires a large amount alike of thought as to its content and of careful expression as to its wording that the language should not demean its subject and thus be productive of an effect opposite to that which is intended. The Chinese are most sensitive to such blunders.' Adding to his difficulty is the need for the proclamation to be 'intelligible' to both the 'populace' and the 'mandarins' (473).

Chase's rendition of the proclamation is again labelled: 'A true translation.' His project is not just linguistic but cultural translation, and he demonstrates both his linguistic skills and cross-cultural access. But the cultural permutations he is so acutely aware of are always in excess of what the words will literally communicate, and can only be rendered as supplements to the translations themselves. This excess, or supplement, is the space which Chase opens up for himself, in his self-identification as cross-cultural agent; it is the space of his participation in the history of empires, his intervention to shape historical decisions and processes. The marginal has become – or so it seems – the hybridised negotiator, travelling between conflictual worlds and discourses, who has the responsibility – and hence the authority – for fostering or breaking communication and directing the course of history. In a much more subtle form than Eastman's cavalier manufacture of photographic records, Chase's efforts underline how history is made of texts and by texts.

But Chase's dedicated attempts at shaping history come up inevitably against the discourses of feudal and imperial hegemony. The indirect result of his first intervention in the dealings between Elliot and Keshen is a Chinese proclamation offering a reward for his death and that of his patron. In the second instance, his culturally sensitive translation of Gough's proclamation is exploited by the General to lull the citizens of Canton into a false sense of security before a devastating bombardment. 'In what sense', Chase asks accusingly in a letter to Gough, 'may the civilian population of the city understand any similar future declarations from the leader of the British Expedition other than as cynical and heartless pleasantries?' (475). In Chase's implicit lament at his loss of credibility, the novel, as a critique of how history is made, retreats from any valorising of the marginal and hybrid and his strategies of discourse which transgress the given boundaries of race, culture and empire. The Chinese and British reactions enact the closure of history by violence, and reconsign Chase to the outer limits of powerlessness. Chase's experience embodies the novel's crucial distinction between the forms of power that control the making of history. History, far from being the space which is open to representation, narrative and discursive exchange, reasserts itself as violent performances of myths of race and empire.

As we have seen, in its own narratorial method and the substance of its critique, *An Insular Possession* resists the notion of history as a master narrative produced by a dominant discourse. The narrative, as I have pointed out, is an interaction of letters, journalistic articles, dialogue and third-person narration. It exposes the constructed or fictional nature of history – an appropriate theme for a historical novel, or a metahistorical or pseudo-historical novel in the late twentieth century. From *Vanity Fair* to *War and Peace*, the nineteenth-century epical novel – which *An Insular Possession* pastiches – recognises the distinction between history and fiction and uses history as resource for the story-teller to interpret more or less accurately. However, for *An Insular Possession*, the boundaries between history and fiction are deliberately blurred; the novel scrutinises the ways in which history is an ongoing dialogue between different forms of records and ideologies, and the potential this offers to peripheral characters for shaping the processes and production of history, and inscribing their own points of view. History, any history of the period (in the words of the *Lin Tin Bulletin*, speaking in another context) 'must be an unfinished story, not a rounded tale' (523). *An Insular Possession* is one of the most recent versions of this 'unfinished story' of the colonising of Hong Kong – in its critique of older forms of telling the story, its imagination of a hitherto unrecognised marginal, American perspective, and its shifting ideological alignments and underpinnings. At the same time, it continues to point towards a history that is unfolding elsewhere, in the domain of the gunboats that enact periodical closures upon ideological and textual negotiations. 'The only end, Gid, is death' (575), remarks Eastman in the final chapter of the novel – trite, yes, but also true.

In all its discourse strategies – direct speech, the epistle, journalese, or third-person narration – *An Insular Possession* imitates and re-creates the idiom of a previous age, familiar to readers of novels such as *Vanity Fair*. But the idiom, written in the present tense, is, of course, a contemporary fantasy, made by craft like the characters, events and the fiction of a third-party history. As a twentieth-century redaction of a nineteenth-century historical novel, *An Insular Possession* participates in the postmodern exchange of realism and fantasy, and shares its currency of playful generic transformation. Realism and fantasy are folded into one another – rather than counterpointed – throughout the novel, and this discursive interaction situates the novel intertextually as much with *Midnight's Children* as with *Vanity Fair*. Such interaction is once again emphasised in the final narrative strategy, the use of appendices at the end of the novel.

'Appendix I' consists of entries from '*A Gazetteer of Place Names and Biographies Relative to the Early China Coast* by An Old Hand', which is supposed to be published in Shanghai in 1935 (577). The second appendix contains passages from a book, *The Morning of My Days*, authored by 'Professor G. H. Chase' (586). In traditional historiographic scholarship, such appendices help to authenticate the account that precedes them, and this is no doubt the function the novel's appendices are meant to imitate and pastiche. While the work cited in 'Appendix II', like its author, is more clearly fictional, 'Appendix I' brings into focus a number of enigmatic exchanges between fact and fiction, realism and fantasy and, furthermore, draws the reader into its ludic process – and, by extension, that of the novel – by placing her/him in an unconscionable position as arbitrator.

First of all, the truth status of '*A Gazetteer*' is highly questionable. It has the semblance of the real; and indeed, among the entries taken from it are the names of real places and people, just as the characters, Captain Elliot and the Chinese Commissioners Lin and Keshen, for instance, in the novel proper are historical persons. Prominent among the entries under 'C' is a short biography of 'Chase, Professor Gideon Hall', enclosed by references to 'Caine, Colonel William' and 'Chek Chu' (578-9). The two latter names are historically verifiable: Caine was a governor of colonial Hong Kong, and Chek Chu is the trans-literation of the Chinese name of a fishing village, also known as Stanley, that even now exists, albeit much gentrified, on the south side of Hong Kong island. The truth status of these two names seeps into that of Chase, mystifying it with the aura of verity. Eastman is not among the list of entries, but his name poses a problem – and a temptation – of another kind. In the novel, he is the one to acquire the rudimentary know-how of early photography, to use such know-how to augment verbal reports and, as we have seen, to manufacture news itself. This fictional nineteenth-century photography enthusiast bears the same surname as the actual nineteenth-century American photography enthusiast who was to invent the Kodak camera and to found Eastman Kodak. It is as if Mo is challenging his reader *not* to wonder naively – just for a moment – whether the two might be related. In this way, Eastman figures as another signpost of the intersections between the real and the make-believe that tantalise and tease.

The reader may be tempted to verify the existence of the gazetteer, the sources of the entries of real historical persons and places, and perhaps even to try and locate the real-life models of

Chase and Eastman. Tempted, yes; but to proceed to do so would be an attempt to determine what is fact and what is fiction, separate the real from the fantastical, and thus to fall precisely into the novel's ludic trap which is set up to subvert established boundaries between the two. It would also be an attempt to enact closures upon the debates about the mimetic, which it is the project of the novel to re-imagine and carnivalise. Tantalised, teased, tempted, the reader is invited instead to embrace such processes and the pleasure of her/his reading, and in doing so, to enter into community with the choric voices of *An Insular Possession* as postmodern novel.[10]

Although much of the novel can be seen as a challenge to and critique of orthodox discourses, there are aspects of its strategy, especially in the doubling of past and present, that are troubling and even self-defeating. As I have mentioned before, there is little about the novel, from its cast of characters to its subliminal critique of historiography, that is constructed as authentically oriental. This in itself is not a problem for in this and other novels, Mo is patently uninterested in the nativist fictions of identity or projects of postcolonial cultural reconstruction and retrieval that characterise the novels of other writers with whom he is sometimes placed in uneasy community.[11] Nor is *An Insular Possession* an investment in the postcolonial narrative of victimhood which confronts and seeks redress for the historical injuries wrought by imperialism upon its others. What is problematic is not the minimal presence of Chinese characters and the Chinese community in Mo's novel but their hackneyed representation. They are disheartening stereotypes, made up of inscrutable speakers of pidgin, alternately xenophobic and abject in their interaction with outsiders. In this respect, the novel looks backwards at an Orientalist tradition of caricature which it simply reanimates and does not challenge. Ironically, it is here that the novel is aligned with an outmoded imperialist and Orientalist discourse, and its revisionist historiographic agenda disrupted.

In making this observation, however, it is not my intention to point to some authentic Chineseness against which Mo's representations are measured and found wanting. There are a number of related issues which are at stake here. First of all, the representations of the Chinese as ethnic subjects in *An Insular Possession* lack the kind of fictional frame that is crucial to locating them in a specific space and time. Such location is the achievement of *Sour Sweet* in which Mo takes on board one of the activities that stereotypes the Chinese immigrant – that they all work in the catering trade – and constructs from it a narrative of immigrant subjectivities. In the earlier novel, as we have seen, 'Chineseness' is explained in terms of a number of cultural practices and kinship and social values; these are, in turn, traced back to Lily's own identity formation in her rural childhood. *Sour Sweet* is largely concerned with the retrenchment of these so-called ethnic traits in a condition of diaspora where Lily finds herself and her family. That such retrenchment perpetuates racialised thinking about self and other, and closes down any cross-boundary or transgressive possibilities, is the paradox of the novel. It is also the measure of Mo's ironic distance from Lily, and his perspective on the replacement of ethnicity in the diaspora.

'Chineseness' in *Sour Sweet* is an identity formation that has a specific temporal–spatial location that precludes it from slipping into generalised abstraction, essentialistic character, or a tired rehearsal of motley stereotypes. But such is not the case with *An Insular Possession*, in which there are very few Chinese characters of dramatic significance, and those who appear are either mandarins of the inscrutable Chinese variety or gaggles of peasants engaged in activities that mystify the expatriates in the novel as much as they did Christopher Isherwood more than half a century ago in *Journey to a War* (1939). No doubt this has to do with the assignment of narrative modalities in the novel: 'Chineseness' is mediated by expatriate observers and narrators who are, in turn, trapped within the discourses of imperialism of their time. However, it is certainly arguable that over the question of representing Chinese people, *An Insular Possession* has forsaken its revisionist, late twentieth-century agenda in the interest of consistency to its nineteenth-century idiom. Whether as deliberate choice or omission, this sounds a discordant note in a novel which seeks to rewrite history from a full awareness of history's fictionalities.

Apart from the dubious representation of the Chinese as ethnic subjects, an expatriate character like Eastman also noticeably replicates nineteenth-century novelistic types of the gentleman–maverick. *An Insular Possession* is written like a nineteenth-century novel, in an idiom which attempts, almost heroically, to conjure the past in the present in order to fulfil what Mo has called a *'sincere* representation'. Much as one may applaud the intention and register the effort, it is impossible, in the end, to read *An Insular Possession* as if it were a nineteenth-century novel. It is by no means clear that *An Insular Possession* is self-consciously aware of the different – and conflictual – ideological implications of the dual processes in the postmodern project of pastiche. To what extent is the novel a project of imitation – with nineteenth-century novels as referential models – and to what extent is it mimicking, and so radically revising, its literary inheritance? The novel has fallen into the gap between imitation and mimicry; 'sincerity' is an emotive invocation which seeks to address the complex lineage of the novel as historical fiction but it cannot really subsume the formal problems of characterisation and the predicament of the novel's reception which come with the re-situation of that lineage in the late twentieth century. In a sense, Mo might be seen to have fallen victim to his own powers of imitation.

An insular possession provides the title of Mo's narrative. But Hong Kong has no presence in the novel as community or culture, except in the final moments as the haven or retreat of foreigners displaced from one trading outpost to another. Almost all the story takes place in the city of Canton in the Qing empire, the Portuguese colony of Macao, and the Pearl River which connects the two. In the narrative, Hong Kong's identity is predicated on its history, on its coming into being as a colonial possession; the moment the city comes into being in the narrative is the moment of colonisation. But very soon after that moment, the narrative closes around it. The insular possession is given no story.

But Hong Kong haunts the narrative of none other than Chase himself. When, near the end of the novel, Chase speaks up against the injustice allowed by the authorities of the new colony, he does so in a private letter which has no public effect. His voice in the public sphere, in the newspaper which he helps to found, also falls silent. The causes which the newspaper has fought for – opposing the opium trade, greater contact between British and Chinese – have all been defeated, and the newspaper ceases publication. Chase is a loser in his story, a marginal figure whose voice goes unheeded by either of the mighty opposites who are making history above his head. He has been a profitable instrument in the hands of the British when he has been used as interpreter in negotiations, but in the end, no one is interested in what he is, either as a mediator of cultures, or as one with opinions of his own. Hong Kong is largely absent from a novel which breaks the promise of its title, and its return through Chase is given a particularly ironical twist at the end of the novel when Chase speaks up against the early colonial administration. Through Chase, Hong Kong *is* given a non-imperial voice, but it is only that of an outsider and loser. In the novel, Hong Kong is spoken for by the contending forces of empire which have reified it as property and the spoils of war; its subject position, if any, is articulated by the enfeebled voice of dissent in a last gasp of illusory agency.

The nation and its others:
The Redundancy of Courage[1]

*T*HE *Redundancy of Courage* narrates the recent history of the
fictional island of Danu which resembles East Timor. Published
in 1991, this novel about an apparently lost cause anticipated the
attention of the global media on Timorese resistance against
Indonesian hegemony in 1996 when two East Timor activists,
Catholic Bishop Carlos Ximenes Belo and Jose Ramos-Horta
won the Nobel Peace Prize, not to mention the more recent
return of Timor to the headlines.[2] Once again, Mo shows how his
artistic antennae are finely tuned to the faintly heard messages
of crisis before they explode on the world's stage.[3] *Redundancy*
is a powerful narrative performance, marshalling and driving
issues and themes which have been migrating and mutating in
the earlier novels. Sometimes the transformation has been
effected by vertiginous reversals of perspective – between, for
instance, Chinese identity as daily reality and imaginary community, history as empire and from the margins. The internal
struggles of the family as community in the first two novels are
displaced and replaced by the struggles between nation-states in
An Insular Possession. Redundancy moves the struggle between
nation-states to the late twentieth century, in order to explore
the transformations which have taken place in imperialism and
colonialism as these global forces continue to frame, define, and
regulate the history and identity of new nations. As it narrates
the struggles between Danu and the other nation-states which
are its enemies and others, *Redundancy* also tells the story of
Danu as nation-community, or, in other words, as a complex

organism which bears the traits of the family-community in *The Monkey King* and *Sour Sweet*, and yet has developed quasi-kinship lineages and horizontal relations that go beyond it.

In his seminal work, *Imagined Communities*, Benedict Anderson declares: 'Communities are to be distinguished, not by their falsity/genuineness, but by the style in which they are imagined.'[4] In this chapter, I will discuss, first of all, the question of Danu in relation to its external others, the powerful imperial nation-states who impose upon it an identity and history as colony. Much of the novel deals with the formation of a Danuese identity in terms of its difference from these external others. The second aspect of this chapter's discussion focuses on how, as an imagined union, a nation-community, a nation-state and a resistant collective, Danu is characterised fraternally and through ambivalent relations with its internal others, notably the protagonist and first-person narrator, Adolph Ng, and the Danuese women activists who fit uneasily into the fraternal and masculinist bonds that guarantee comradeship. In interviews before and after the publication of the novel, Mo has confessed that he found the writing of *Redundancy* arduous, not least because of his dislike for Adolph Ng.[5] While the more thought-ful reviews draw attention to the fascinating ambivalence in the choice of Ng and his positioning as narrator, there has also been hostile questions about his credibility and authority to speak of and for a war of resistance. Thus, the third issue which this chapter will discuss, and which inevitably folds into the previous two, is the dubious empowerment of Adolph Ng as the narrator of Danu.

Redundancy relocates the issues of identity and history in the late twentieth-century struggle between nation-states and, through the quasi-allegory of Timorese resistance, puts an urgent postcolonial spin on these issues. The postcolonial discourse in *Redundancy* maps the project of nation-building and the making of the national subject onto that of resistance against neo-colonialism. These projects, which also mark the crucial transi-tions in Danu's recent history and identity formation, are made and unmade as Danu struggles against an overlapping succession of predatory others who act in complicity and collusion. In the novel, Danu gains independence from Portugal only to be quickly recolonised by its newly independent neighbour, the nation-state of *malai* ethnics, whose military forces move in to fill the space vacated by European imperialism. This act of aggression has the implicit sanction of American capital which is keen to exploit Danu's offshore oil reserves, and which sees Danu's fledgling socialist government as hostile to its global interests. For Danu, colonialism is the immediate past and imminent future; the nation-state becomes that in-between space of combat, crisis and emergency, and nationalism becomes the ideology of resistance. But in *malai* aggression against Danu, the imperialistic will of the new nation-state represents the betrayal of nationalism as liberationist ideology. This double move telescopes the historical time and space of postcolonial fictional discourse for the last fifty years since the mid-twentieth century. It encompasses, first, an earlier period of decolonisation when fiction celebrates the nation-state and justifies it in invented traditions, and second, more recent moments when nationalism appears as a suspect ideology, and nation-states are seen as the sites of hegemonic and neo-colonial practices. In a third and further complication, the narrative of the Danuese nation situates *Redundancy* in the terrain of postcolonial fiction in the late twentieth century by showing how the nationalist project is co-opted by the interests of global capital and, through the world media, incorporated into the political and cultural preoccupations of the developed western world.[6]

Redundancy is memorable for its detailed scenes of combat and violence which confirm, once again, Mo's gift for action-writing we have seen in the excruciating gang-fights of *Sour Sweet* and the battlefields of *An Insular Possession*. The novel begins with an account of the *malai* invasion, and in his attention to the atrocities as they unfold, Adolph Ng is an excellent eyewitness, an irresistible reminder of the struggle between nations as a conflict of bodies, a life-and-death struggle from which the abstract or the emblematic offers no escape. The bombing and maiming of the Danuese capital by the invaders, 'piles of bodies in the streets' (9), 'the *malais* who ... felled [Sonia] with a back-handed slash of the gun-butt against the jaw' (21) – from an overview of the carnage to its most brutal instance, Ng observes and reports with a mixture of horror and fascination. Right from the beginning of the invasion, the voice of Danu to the outside world usually embodied in the Australian journalist Mabbeley is silenced when he is shot by the *malais* (22). The death of the journalist of conscience inaugurates the novel's rejection of the media as the narrators of Danuese resistance, and the perspective of Adolph Ng, who enjoys dubious privilege as Danuese national and eyewitness, and who also, in his own words at a moment of observation, 'enjoyed all the sensations of the voyeur' (16).

Developing Benedict Anderson's idea of 'nation-ness' as 'cultural artefacts of a particular kind',[7] Homi Bhabha has discussed how nations are artificial constructs like narratives, and more significantly, constructed *as* narratives.[8] In two episodes in *Redundancy* (Chapters Eight and Twenty-five), Ng watches the conflicts between Danu and its *malai* invaders as a contest for the power to narrate, and the control of those media of narration that could determine the outcome of the contest. The silencing of Mabbeley develops into full-blown cynicism about the western media, and their credibility as witness to truth. The Australian film crew who arrive to report the invasion are shot dead by the *malais*, who then reported the film crew to be the victims of a bomb planted by the Danuese leaders, the FAKOUM. This episode has a further, and salutary, lesson for Ng: 'From the start,' he says, 'our fate was determined not by ourselves, not locally or by the invader even, but abroad, in Canberra and Washington' (110). The competition between the two versions of events is arrested, not by any resolution of the truth, but because a change of government from Labour to Liberal in Australia put an end to further investigations. At the same time, *malai* disinformation portrays the Danuese leaders as dangerous communists whose regime subverts the stability of the region, thus justifying the invasion especially to the Cold War sensitivities of the United States. In a later episode, a group of western journalists, invited by Mrs Goreng, the *malai* commander's wife, arrive to report on the condition of the pacified Danu. Ng, by this time a captive of the *malais* and a functionary in Mrs Goreng's entourage, observes them with increasing, though silent, contempt as their 'group comportment' deteriorates (358), and the journalists behave like 'spoiled kids' endlessly complaining about the facilities they are offered. The novel's critique of the western media moves to a climax which is as nuanced as it is devastating, as Ng reports the disjunction between a journalist's personal and professional recognition:

> Just before they left, Speich called me to his room... 'You like me to take a letter to any friend? Or a message for anyone – anyone you know?'
>
> I knew what he was saying. I did trust him... But I didn't like the terrible risk. 'No, *tuan*,' I said. He looked at me and understood. I didn't think I saw condemnation in his eyes. I turned at the door and said, 'Just write the truth, *tuan* Hans, that will be the message.' It was what I'd said to Bill Mabbeley.
>
> Speich said, 'Truth is relative, Mr Ng. Like beauty it is in the eye of the beholder.' (359)

Against the powerful circuit of *malai* disinformation and self-interested western reception which generates the narrative of Danu, the journalist's private conscience and professional commitment to truth have been, for Ng, a single and inimitable point of departure towards a counter-narrative. But as the quotation shows, while conscience remains visible as an interpersonal ethic, it has been severed from the commitment to truth in the journalist's relations with the wider world for which he is supposed to bear witness, and to which he is supposedly accountable.

From the slaughterhouse of dead and dismembered bodies, and with the western media either silenced or discredited, Ng steps diffidently forward as the narrator of Danu. We can see right from the beginning that as story-teller, Ng's forte is his eye for detail. The novel opens with the scenes of the *malai* invasion; while the nation – literally and figuratively – disintegrates around him, Ng can only focus on the minutiae of his surroundings. 'It's the small things which can bring about the greatest sense of violation'(10), he says. As the bombs fall from the sky, 'my whole world had come down to tiny things,' he observes, 'the flies, the seeds, a few blades of grass, a couple of pebbles. They started to assume a momentous significance for me' (12). As the observer, recorder and narrator of Danu's history, Ng's optical field is the micro-real, at the other extreme from that hyperreality concocted by the western media complicit with the political interests of the west and compliant to western tastes and partisan concerns.[9] *Redundancy* entrusts the narrative (and hence the memory) of Danu to Ng in preference to the greater, and grandiose, power of the foreign media; it is Ng's reportage which is the novel. If the conflict between nations materialises, in cultural terms, as a contest of narratives, Ng's narration raises a lone voice against both *malai* hegemony and the arrogant self-interests of the west. Writing Danu's history as the rise of the autonomous nation-state and anti-colonial resistance rather than as national defeat and colonial subjection, Ng's narrative remembers and re-members a nation broken and disjointed by conquest.

As the voice of resistance, Ng is paradoxically hesitant, cowardly, non-committal. To understand this paradox generically, and within the postcolonial turn which *Redundancy* enacts, is to relocate the traditional epic in this late twentieth-century moment long after the modernist narrative, as in Conrad's *Lord Jim* and Joyce's *Ulysses*, has made it impossible to imagine the heroism of epic unironically.[10] The voice of Adolph Ng articulates the satiric epic of the nation as postmodernist genre. Ng is the eyewitness participant and sole narrator of Danu's history, and as such, assumes the role of the bard in traditional epic whose narrative remembers and enshrines heroism, and engenders the nation's founding myths. But his voice, ambivalent and sometimes frankly whining, also unsettles the bardic inflections of traditional epic which register identification with, rather than difference from, the values of heroism being narrated. In the grounding of this ambivalent voice, the narrative announces its intra-national discourse; Ng's difference from the heroic others he narrates is explained and justified in terms of the ethnic complexities of Danu. In his next novel, *Brownout on Breadfruit Boulevard*, Mo's representation of the Philippines will be divided into two equal parts, between the lives and perspectives of the natives, and those of foreigners and temporary visitors. *Redundancy* makes space for the outside – not only invaders but also marginals like Ng in the national community – as it becomes incorporated inside, into the unfolding history of Danu.

Both *The Monkey King* and *Sour Sweet* problematise Chinese ethnicity – its stereotypes and the conditions under which they are formed – from the perspective of protagonists situated on the margins of majority Chinese communities. In these two novels, the imaginations of 'Chineseness' in different times and places can be seen as an ethnic inflection of the paradigm of identity in current postmodernist and postcolonial discourses. *An Insular Possession*, as we have seen, occludes 'Hong Kong' as Chinese community, and narrates instead the founding of the city as a British colony. *Redundancy* moves further to displace Chineseness from Mo's artistic pre-occupations. Despite the Chinese ancestry of the first-person narrator, Adolph Ng, the novel has no investment in questions of 'Chineseness' in the diaspora. Its central concerns are with nations as they emerge from colonial histories – how they are built, what forms they take, what problems they confront. Ethnicities in contact and conflict are very much the stuff of modern nation-building and national formations after colonialism;[11] if Mo is interested in ethnicity in *Redundancy*, it is as a constituent in the discourse of the nation.

Nation-building is an heroic enterprise, often conceived on the grandest scales, mobilising multitudes, cutting across the divisions of the brave and the cowardly, the wise and the fool-hardy, the imaginative and the pragmatic, in a collective project perceived as emancipatory and legitimising. The rhetoric of nationhood, in its recurrent references to bonds of kinship, common lineage and single origins, and its exhortation to physical action and sacrifice, speaks often of the body – as organic entity, in states of disease and health, both functioning and dysfunctional. The rhetoric of the body and of sacrifice permeates nineteenth-century romanticist and organicist conceptions of the nation. Ernest Renan, for instance, speaks of a 'large aggregate of men, healthy in mind and warm of heart, [which] creates the kind of moral conscience which we call a nation. So long as this moral consciousness gives proof of its strength by the sacrifices which demand the abdication of the individual to the advantage of the community, it is legitimate and has the right to exist.'[12] The island of Danu is a body with a history: from colonised infancy (and impotency) to independence and maturity. The body stands up for itself and is then afflicted with an infestation of foreign bodies – the *malais*; the nation falls ill. It is invaded by a pathology, becomes diseased, endures pain, develops resistance; the island-nation is a body as a site of contestation, threatened with death. As the Danuese leaders transform into guerrilla fighters with Ng as their reluctant armaments expert in charge of bombs and booby traps, the nation takes further shape as the physical site where bodies impact on each other, and are mangled by weapons, machinery and technology. This material embodiment of the nation constitutes a narrative discourse which runs parallel to and against the imagination of the nation as symbolic and political entity. The body is both a metonymy for the nation and the place where its materiality is made present and tangible.

Nation-building is also the element of the individual as hero, throwing up historical subjects whose capacity for achieving the impossible translates as commonly into leadership as into sacrifice. In literary history, the fictional genre of nation-building is undeniably the epic. Striding and thrusting their way through narratives of martial valour and tumultuous action, epical heroes are the grandest of literary archetypes. Achilles, Ulysses, Aeneas, Milton's Satan (whom one might see as the founder of a separatist nation): in their epical figuration, it is their powerful, muscular bodies which mark them out as heroes, bodies that do not flinch under pain, that seem impervious to privation and hardship, that tower above the swarming and heaving masses of common humanity.

Like his loyalty to the resistance which is always in doubt, Ng's commitment to the heroic tenor of his narrative vacillates from moment to moment. His perspective on heroism, though detailed and informed by knowledge of his location, is also constricted; necessitated by crisis, this constricted perspective is also symptomatic of his character – or failure of character – in the novel. He can rarely turn his eyes away from immediate pain and pleasure to imagine the broad vision and sweep of ambition which empower the enterprise of resistance, and transform ordinary people into heroes and heroines. In its exclusive investment in Ng's perspective, the novel also underlines his inalienable difference from his peers. In this respect, *Redundancy* continues Mo's exploration of how cultures, entirely discrete from each other, are forced into contact and alignment, except that, unlike *An Insular Possession*, *Redundancy* shows this accidental encounter and conflict of differences not between east and west but within the formation of a single nation-state. Ng, the embodiment of a particular subject and culture in Danu, becomes, by force of circumstance, the historian of his Danuese other, or those of his compatriots engaged in a heroic project which he is temperamentally unsuited to, and a nationalist resistance he has no wish to join. How can that be done? The first-person narrative, which is the answer to this question, invents the possibility of a history written by an insider who is also outside, swinging between identity and difference as Ng looks at himself and his supposed comrades. It is this in-betweenness which makes him both an astute and unreliable narrator.

Throughout the novel, Ng addresses the reader in confiding and intimate tones. But the register of intimacy is unsettled by a cynical voice which derides itself: 'My name is Adolph Ng. Please laugh. To pronounce it, imagine you have been constipated a long time. Now strain. There you have my surname' (24). The invitation to identify his name in terms of bodily function, or in this case dysfunction, locates Ng within the tradition of the satiric subject. Satire, whether classical or Swiftian, has always found in the body, its parts, states, and frequently its supposedly basest functions, a rich source of what is laughable and absurd about the human condition.[13] In this light, Ng's dysfunctional body does not speak of the grandeur of his bardic position but its absurdity, and in openly inviting the readers to laugh at him, Ng also cultivates their appetite for the absurd, and the bond between narrator and reader in a satirical critique of nationhood and resistance.

In a further twist, Ng trains his, and the reader's, satiric eye on his own dubious ethnicity. He has a Chinese surname and insists on representing himself as ethnically overdetermined. In his self-description, he is 'of Chinese race', and characterised by what he calls 'Chinese pragmatism' (24) through and through. But ethnicity, and specifically Chinese ethnicity, in the novel, is hardly the sign of valour or communal affiliation. Ng draws attention recurrently to his own abject cowardice and impure motives. Even when he later achieves some success in devising and planting landmines against the *malai* invaders, he describes his expertise as 'peculiarly Chinese … in its ingenuity, in its low small-mindedness, its attention to detail, its pettyfogging neatness' (168). Right from the start, he has little sense of community, either with the diasporic Chinese community of Danu or the native and *mestizo* nationalist. In a moment of crisis, as on the day of the *malai* invasion, he seeks refuge in the Chinese quarter, only to turn his back on it. Furthermore, 'Chineseness' makes sense only as difference from *mestizo* and native Danuese, and this difference is the product of inherited and opposite orientations of their communities. A second generation Danuese of Chinese descent, Ng begins school in the Catholic seminary on the island where he formed early friendships with the *mestizos* who would later form the core of the national government and resistance against the *malais*. But unlike them, who continue their education in Danu and then Portugal, Ng leaves Danu to attend private high school in another Portuguese colony, Macao, which has a majority Chinese community. Though still the beneficiary of Portuguese colonial education, Ng makes an early passage to what lies outside of Danu; when he goes to university in Canada rather than Portugal to study engineering, his connections with Danu are further attenuated.

Ng's *mestizo* friends mark him off by the derisory label 'Chinaman', but what separates them, besides ethnicity, is that the *mestizo* passage outwards has a definite ideological and political orientation which is absent from Ng's largely pragmatic education. As students and colonial ethnics in the so-called 'mother-country', the *mestizo* passage outwards to Portugal does not take them far from Danu; it only serves to confirm them as anti-colonialists, and as place and political commitment, Danu remains the location of their identity. Ng's 'Chineseness' places him outside of the Danuese nation as it is constituted by the *mestizo* as an organic community founded on ethnic ties. At the same time, his educational trajectory, which promotes functional rather than political training and the career goals to go with it, compounds his alienation. The *mestizos* are cultural and political Danuese nationalists,[14] and against their unitary construct of the nation, Ng's 'Chineseness' is the sign of difference and ambivalence. Paradoxically, it is also as 'Chinese' that Ng becomes identified and located in Danu:

> Now I had found an identity, a place in the little society of Danu. It was not quite what I had desired, but there was no question that was how I was seen. I was a Chinese entrepreneur with capital. I was an exploiter. I was a provider of work. I was a parasite. I was hated. I was to be appeased. I was vulnerable. I was powerful. This was interesting. (51)[15]

Ng further complicates this alienated and imposed 'Chinese' position with a sense of his own deterritorialisation as he describes himself recurrently as a 'citizen of the world'. Facile though the description may seem, it is the easy way for Ng to signal his alternative position outside the corporeal nation-community of Danu; he is not to be defined by what he is – a 'Chinese' – or where he is (after all, where is 'the world'?) but by where he is not, that is, Danu. Neither ethnic ancestry nor a specific geographical location are constituents in an individual's self-identification, all the more because they have become the means by which identity is imposed from the outside in a process of stereotyping, discrimination and marginalisation. In taking on this nebulous identity of 'citizen of the world', Ng implicitly positions himself for his role as Danu's historian and narrator in place of the foreign media whose purview, it would seem, is 'the world', and whose optic situates the 'little society of Danu' in it. Who better to perform this role than Ng, who can claim to know Danu because he has a place in it given and acknowledged by others, and who, at the same time, is 'of the world' like the global media. In other words, he is both the cosmopolitan modernist subject and has a kind of locus in the postcolonial nation.

Homi Bhabha has asked: 'If the ambivalent figure of the nation is a problem of its transitional history, its conceptual indeterminacy, its wavering between vocabularies, then what effect does this have on narratives and discourse that signify a sense of "nationness"?'.[16] In Ng's satiric self-positioning, and the *mestizo*'s derogatory label, being 'Chinese' is the sign of a dysfunctional body, anti-nation, unbelonging, and the unheroic. Ng the ethnic is the parody of the nation, if nation is seen, as it is by the *mestizo* nation-builders and later resistance fighters, as epic. His body is that of the laughable clown – grotesque, heavy, soft and importunate – discomfited both by pleasure and pain. It also signals an alternative sexuality, disaffiliating him from the men of the nation who always show, as he notices, 'a slight unease' (35) in his company. With women, his relationship is 'limpid' (35); but they are marginalised like himself, and indeed his narrative pays them scant attention in contrast to the male leadership, especially Osvaldo Oliveira.

Significantly, the novel begins with the murder by the *malais* of Sonia Ferreira, lover of Osvaldo, recognised by Ng as 'the real driving force behind FAKOUM, its true as opposed to titular leader' (18). In the mapping of nation and gender communities, it has been observed that 'like gender … nationality is a relational term whose identity derives from its inherence in a system of differences'.[17] The Danuese nation, constituted of its male and masculinist leaders, identifies itself not only against the ethnically separate 'Chinaman', but also against the differently gendered. Like Ng, the female body is forcibly incorporated into the virile fraternity of the Danuese nation, and suffers different forms of degendering. Of the two named women in the Danuese core-leadership, the first, Rosa Soares, is described as a tough, pugnacious and betel-chewing descendent of headhunters, who has no interest in men. This makes for her special bond with Ng who is very interested. The second, the physician Maria Nolasco da Silva, 'utterly Chinese in appearance' (33), is, to Ng, the one most true to the ideals of nationhood but who also pays the savage price of being raped by Danu's invaders.

As the women cross the ethnic and gender divides within Danu, and become agents in the process of nation-building and resistance, their ethnic and gendered subjectivities also become incorporated into the masculinist nationalist body. This incorporation translates their condition of ethnic and gender in-betweenness into a loss of identity where they can neither be fully themselves nor the other. And when internal colonisation is doubled and forcibly enacted on their bodies by the colonising *malais*, this loss materialises in their violation, and ultimately in death. Despised for his ethnicity, homosexuality and effeminate cowardliness, Ng stands in affinity and solidarity with the women, and it is his friendship with them which guarantees his voicing of their experience. As colleague or colonised subject, Ng's bond with the women implicitly critiques the nation identified as exclusively male, but the space of the women's multifaceted heroism in his narrative is very marginalised. For the most part, the story of Danu, narrated by Adolph Ng, remains very much a 'boys' own' territory, as it dwells, un-heroically, on the antics of the male leaders during the various momentous transitions of history. Though sycophantic, his relationship with Mrs Goreng bears traits of his earlier friendly intimacy with the women guerrillas. Brusque, wily and manipulative, Mrs Goreng is a latter-day Lily Chen, a favourite Mo woman-type, equipped with the charms exercised by a woman self-consciously cultivating and exploiting her place in a man's world, empowered because of her subscription and access to male domination, and powerless because of her dependency and subjection under men.

Ng's body is the body of pathos or even ridicule, but significantly it is also the body of satire, for its acute awareness of its own absurdity issues in mockery of the kinetic language of others, seeing, for example, the radicals in their early nationalist phase as 'jutting-jaw Lenins' (66), and later as 'military adventurers, frizzy-haired Napoleons' (68), whose bodies betray them into unconscious truth-telling. At Danu's Independence Day celebrations, the narrator's satiric eye registers those elements that are discordant with the spectacle of nationhood. This is the Danuese nation's originary moment; as national subject, Ng is drawn into it sufficiently to note that 'it turned out to be not only a moving but also a disciplined spectacle', and as bardic commentator, he insists that 'nothing the *malai* did could blot out that memory' (97). But as satirist, Ng also irreverently discomposes the spectacle of the nation as a disciplined body. He registers how parts of the body have, literally, escaped discipline: Arsensio, one of the national leaders, 'had two days' growth to go with the reflective shades' (95). And then 'all the stamping and swaying' of bodies moving in the rhythm of the national anthem turns farcical as the motion causes grenades left on the leaders' podium to move, to start 'to tremble, then rock, and finally roll this way and that'. Epic is invaded by satire, the ceremony of nationhood stirs up a carnival rock and roll. Thrown into confusion, Ng exclaims:

> I really wasn't sure what to do. I mean, really, I figured it was better to be blown up than interrupt 'O, Mighty Mountain!' Osvaldo caught my eye, threw his head back, shot out his chest and joined in the chorus with gusto. I also made my mouth move, not wanting to be a suspect Chinaman (there were few enough of us attending in all conscience). But I couldn't help allowing my eyes to stray downwards. Those rolling bombs, they mesmerised. Always quick, Osvaldo realised what I was thinking, and still singing lustily, flicked a grenade off the table with his fingernail… In all honesty I couldn't say I'd ever found that Osvaldo had the greatest sense of humour but he had me that time. What a time and place, too. Son of a bitch. (96)

The nation is literally on shaky ground, poised, at its founding moment, on the brink of destruction. Ng refocuses the satiric lens on the nation as spectacle and community as collective performance. Both Ng and Osvaldo are actors and performers, but Osvaldo transforms effortlessly into stage-manager while Ng sinks back into the immobility of the captive audience. Osvaldo is the heroic body in the nation conceived as epic. When Ng first catches sight of him, he is running, 'stripped to the waist', 'in good shape', his body 'sinewy', his breathing regular (59). Here, in the quotation, as he throws his head back, shoots out his chest and joins in the chorus of the national anthem with gusto while flicking a grenade off the table with his fingernail, Osvaldo's body motions are seamless, moving without hesitation in between the nation as collective performance and the nation as site of danger. Through Osvaldo, the narrative institutes a postcolonial subject entirely contrary to the 'mesmerised' Adolph Ng.

When the *malai* invasion drives the Danuese leaders into the jungle, Osvaldo resumes his earlier role as leader of the anti-colonial resistance and becomes commander of the guerrillas. Ng is captured by the guerrillas, and finds himself forcibly incorporated into the resistance as the expert on explosives and sabotage. This development is replete with irony, given Ng's self-acknowledged cowardice and the fact that his education as an engineer was supposed to prepare him for a safe and prosperous career. It underlines his subjection to the dynamic of the nation and its unfolding history, and his lack of agency refocuses what we have already seen about the hapless fate of peripheral subjects in *An Insular Possession*. Ng's contingent and groundless identity is thrown into relief by the notion of his personal history as a series of accidents working out against the heroic model of Osvaldo with his self-determination and clear sense of heroic purpose. The narrative of their joined history has a double register in which each interrogates the other: the romantic voice of the nineteenth-century nation-project resonant with timeless and heroic endeavour, and the querulous voice of one who is co-opted by being in the wrong place at the wrong time.

The relation between Osvaldo and Ng is the central theme of the novel, since each in his way – the virile and the importunate, the 'pure' Danuese and the worldly outsider – is a representative body, devoted, one by choice and the other by accident, to Danu. The first-person narrative means that Osvaldo's subjectivity is seen through the eyes of Ng, a strategy Mo successfully exploits to position the two as identity and as alterity. Narrating himself from moment to moment, from one accidental transformation to another, Ng's subjectivity is transient, indeterminate, always in excess of the 'Chinese' frame. Narrated *by* Ng, Osvaldo is often the unified subject, immune to pain, doubt, and even satire: he 'seemed to have consumed all that was comfortable about his own body, and then have discarded it with contempt' (60). A model of heroism is drawn, but what motivates the hero is impenetrable to someone like Ng, the unheroic. The heroes of traditional epics are not problematic to their narrators since they both share wholeheartedly the same set of values. But Osvaldo is a problem to Ng. All he has to go by is what he can see of Osvaldo's behaviour. At times, he speculates on what it portends: 'Outwardly serene, aloof, [Osvaldo] was anything but remote from what was going on underneath him' (208). More often than not, Ng is baffled: 'There were times when Osvaldo asserted himself and there were times when he didn't but his choice of moment always surprised me' (215). Ng's failure to comprehend Osvaldo the strategist, in a guerrilla warfare which demands above all strategic thinking at every point, adds to the mystery of the model hero.

The mystery that is Osvaldo does not entirely inhibit Ng from pointing an occasional finger at what appears to be less than heroic. The obverse of Ng's awe is his satiric ability to puncture Osvaldo's pristine glamour; the knowing voice of the eyewitness narrator is often punctuated by satiric asides as the narrative of the jungle returns again and again to Osvaldo: 'Osvaldo was efficient about anything he'd set his mind to. He was capable of clemency but – how can I put it? – like in one hundred per cent doses. He wasn't a 50–50 liberal. For him the world was black and white...; it was part of his nobility and his baseness, too' (231). Confident assumption can quickly give way to astonishment and incredulity: 'Osvaldo was unafflicted by any false sense of heroism; he appeared utterly unembarrassed by the fact that he was remaining in (comparative!) safety, while perhaps sending his best men to their deaths. I guess he didn't have anything to prove. Lucky guy, don't you think?' (243). Through the rhetorical question, Ng places himself in a community with the reader against Osvaldo, the object of reading; at moments like this, the voice of Ng the guerrilla shades into that of Ng the chronicler and elegist. As he looks back on Osvaldo the character and their shared experiences of resistance, even with the benefit of hindsight, Ng is no more successful in penetrating the core of heroic and epical subjectivity which bears the name of Osvaldo. He says:

> I came to Osvaldo in mid-adventure. I arrived at a moment of no special importance. I departed also at a juncture of little significance. On both occasions, I had prior warning as to the turn my fate would take. Of how little consequence we are. And how difficult it is to accept that startling fact. The great meteors, and I call big O. a great meteor – their fates are bound up with history, their petty accidents act on the levers of events, but the likes of the Corporal, me, even Maria … we could die and nothing would have changed. (309)

A huge chasm is opened between Ng and Osvaldo, self and Other, one in the order of that which separates the earthbound from the superterrestrial 'meteor'. In the domain of history, it is the gulf between the one who has agency, to 'act on the levers of events', and the rest like Ng who have none. In this light, the title of the novel, *The Redundancy of Courage*, which in one sense reads as satiric comment on the pointlessness of Osvaldo's or Danuese resistance, takes on another cast. It embodies the view of history as quasi-providential or at least as the working-out of a determinate scheme of things in which heroic agency is innate to the privileged few, and unknowable to others; these others, like Ng, just do not have it in them to be courageous. Osvaldo is epical precisely because the world he is in is not, and the world he is in is made up mostly of Adolph Ngs. The title, awkward and cumbersome, is as much a comment on the failure of epic, or epical heroism, as an embarrassed apology of the satiric self.

At the end of the narrative, the *malais* are still in occupation; Osvaldo is captured and then killed in an explosion which he arranges himself, and Ng goes into exile to an unknown destination in South America, eventually ending up in Brazil. The history of Danu is unfinished, but the heroic body belongs to the past, dismembered in the cause, while the grotesque anti-heroic body performs the biological functions of survival, and the narrative function of remembering and re-membering Osvaldo, ensuring his survival (though necessarily in an ironic mode). The novel constructs identity between hero and narrator (or bard) in the manner of traditional epic, but also construes their subjective and ideological disjunction. For Ng the exile, narrating is an act of re-placement among those with whom he has once shared – or endured – a past, but it also confirms disaffiliation and exile as the constants in his subjectivity. Ng is alive to write the history of Danu precisely because he is not part of that history, or if he is, it is as difference – the gatecrasher, the defector, the one who got away.

Why then is Ng empowered to speak for Danu? The Australian critic, Ron Blaber, reading Danu as East Timor, finds Ng's narrative authority highly questionable, precisely for those reasons of marginality – his Chinese ethnicity, homosexuality, and dubious commitment to Danuese nationality – which make it impossible for him to share a solidarity of understanding with the others. Thus the focalisation of events through him is idio-syncratic and potentially distorting.[18] Blaber admits that for those like him who are 'familiar with' East Timor, Ng's fictionalised history, refracted by his multiple and marginal subjectivities, raises a further postcolonial question about the ethics of representation. To Blaber, it was highly dubious, if not outright wrong, for Timothy Mo to tell the story in this manner. In another review of *Redundancy*, Tariq Ali, speaking from a similar position of commitment, arrives at a diametrically opposite conclusion. Beginning with the premise – and the curious inversion of signification – that 'East Timor is Danu',[19] Ali goes on to praise the novel for its precise local realities which, in turn, engender types of resistant and oppressive subjects recognisable to readers in disparate postcolonial locations, for example, in Africa or Latin America. The problematic discourse of the first-person narrator, which this chapter has underlined, takes a political turn in the particular contention of these two reviews, but it is a turn which links up with other complications rather than leading to a decisive closure.

Ng's identity as the narrator of Danu's recent history is self-assigned, one he takes on after his own safe departure from the 'pacified' island as a reward for saving the son of the *malai* commander and his wife during a guerrilla attack. The imperative to memorialise is announced right at the beginning of the novel: 'I don't want them forgotten,' he says, 'Rosa, Osvaldo, Raoul, Maria, Martinho, Arsenio. It would be easy to say in the glib way of those who can lead uninterrupted lives in placid places that such oblivion would be a fate worse than death. No fate is worse than death' (3). The first-person narrative is meant to be elegiac rather than confessional, about the roll-call of those whose histories he knows as one of them. The imperative to memorialise also sets in motion an act of conjuration, against that 'death' which is at once physical fact and metaphorical disappearance from the history, recognition, and consciousness of the living.[20] In *An Insular Possession*, we have already seen how Mo tries to remember the Opium War through a non-partisan narrative focalised by Chase and Eastman. Commenting on Adolph Ng, he says, 'I chose the narrator to get the best angle to get into the material and he was the right angle from which to do that.'[21] The choice of narrator for *The Redundancy of Courage* is not driven simply by aesthetic concerns, but is as deliberate and conscionable as the title of the novel itself. If resistance is not possible, courage still is, and Ng survives to record both its value and its waste. But when resistance is not possible, then courage, even as it does exist, is the supplement, that which intervenes in the power of dominant meaning, and yet cannot be meaning itself. Mo leaves the agenda of resistance to nation-as-oppression in the late twentieth century wide open by refusing to commit his novel to either an epical or heroic mode or to privilege Ng the satirist.

Just as the focalisation of narrative through Ng is both revealing and unreliable, Ng's narratorial authority is paradoxically both enhanced and vitiated by his dubious commitment to nation-building or resistance as heroic. In these multiple contradictions, Ng, as elegist and memorialist, refuses to succumb to nostalgia or like Lily Chen, invent an imaginary prelapsarian world of which he remains as guardian. He is a guardian but of a different, and much more striated geography of remembrance: looking back on the past as comedy, farce and satire, he goes against the tragic grain which Osvaldo's death implies, by refusing to turn the nation into a grieving spectacle or the roll-call of names of the dead into a liturgy of absence.[22] He not only sees heroism but also ultimately its defeat, a defeat which, in the sanctuary of his exile, he can but will not pass over in silence. Thus in narrating, in speaking about a past which has remained unspoken, and whose tragic tenor is almost unspeakable, Ng makes an act of commitment against history which seeks to marginalise, ignore and bury this past. Unlike his critic, Mo does not profess to be 'familiar' with East Timor; as with all his novels, even those that deal with material on which he might have claimed an insider perspective, Mo has refused once again, through Adolph Ng, to justify his fictional representation as repository of some kind of authentic or historical truth. His overriding concern, in *Redundancy*, as in *An Insular Possession*, is with the transformation of history into memory, and to demonstrate, through the process of fiction, how this transformation may be effected, and how memory holds forth many possible routings into the past, which centrifugal and partisan histories foreclose and disallow. But memory is also notoriously selective, and therefore, unreliable; in the micro-realism of his narrative, Ng tries to grasp as much of the past, to make it live again as the substance of everyday life at the same time as he maps heroism and its discontents. To enact fiction's contest of hegemonic discourses is not the same as local resistance against colonialism which describes summarily the project of the Timorese fighters; Mo never falls into vulgarising confusion or posits any resemblance between the two. But his novel is an act of solidarity with the real-life referents of his representation, and is recognised as such by readers who do not necessarily agree with Blaber.[23] It endorses, admires, and supports the cause of political and national resistance even as it remains sarcastic, sceptical and dystopic about nationalism as a collective and self-defining project.

Home and the world:
Brownout on Breadfruit Boulevard

BROWNOUT *on Breadfruit Boulevard* is marked by two
momentous departures from Mo's previous work. The first
involves his controversial decision to publish the book privately,
and the second, the breaking off from an established pattern of
character-centred narratives in which the novel unfolds with the
changing experiences of the protagonist figures. Typically, they
are high-risk moves, and, as it often is with Mo, the mixture of
principle and bravura is easy to see, but hard to measure.
Brownout not only throws down the gauntlet to its enemy, the
multinational publishing houses which dominate the market,
but also tries to unsettle potential friends among readers and
critics by refusing to confirm expectations of Mo's practice based
on his previous work. With the publication of *Renegade or
Halo²*, Mo's latest novel to date, it is possible to look back on
Brownout as signalling several changes in direction. Formally
and artistically, this is betrayed by a dilatoriness which plays to
Mo's weaknesses rather than strengths as a writer. But before
discussing this, I will like to talk about the publication controversy and its implications.

The saga of Mo's break from Chatto and Windus, where he
had published his previous two novels, and his row with his
agent, are well chronicled in the literary press, and provided
considerable publicity for the novel. We are told that Mo
initially asked for, and was refused, a £200,000 advance for the
manuscript of *Brownout*. His agent put the manuscript up for
bidding, and Viking's offer of £125,000 was turned down by Mo.

Already frustrated with the way his novels were marketed, and since his manuscript did not elicit offers which he thought acceptable, Mo decided to publish the novel privately through his own – rather whimsically named – Paddleless Press. A more detailed version of the story reported that several publishers who read the manuscript reacted unfavourably to the novel's coprophiliac Prologue, and advised changes.[1] Outrage at what he perceived to be an act of censorship compounded his growing hostility towards the practices of the publishing industry; Mo launched his own private venture.

While it is rare if not unique for an established writer to conduct such an open and rancorous dispute with powerful publishing houses, there is a familiar ring to Mo's story. As we have seen, he had never fought shy of polemic, and this recent episode witnesses how his tendency to provoke has issued not only in invective but, more significantly, in action. The break over *Brownout* is the culmination of a history of publicly expressed discontent over what Mo perceives as unfair dealing on the part of publishers, their unctuous lack of scruple in exploiting creative talent. As early as 1986, when Mo left the publishing house André Deutsch for Chatto and Windus, he declared, 'I'm intolerant, violent, and perfectionist about the publication of my books.' While he considered those involved in editing 'charming', 'the villains, in publishing', he says rather ominously, 'are the ones you never see'.[2] Two years later, he was much more forthright about these 'villains':

> Two publishers have asked me to have lunch. They are interested in my next book. Standard publishing ploy. They want to make me love them so much they can pay me less money. Publishers like to personalise things so they can manipulate the authors better: loyalty, trust are invoked. Actually, not the smallest shred of sentiment influences a company's attitude to its writers. They will drop them if it suits, but you are not meant to behave like that. Novelists, mostly, are by definition shrewd enough to realise this but most do not have the spine to stand up. As far as I am concerned, the man and woman I am eating

with are confidence tricksters... I think publishers are
used-car salesmen with plums in their mouths.[3]

Characteristically scathing – and colourful – in his dismissal of
publishers, Mo also takes writers to task for their lack of 'spine',
a condition which is all the more complicitous because they are
'shrewd enough' to know they are being exploited and mani-
pulated. In the light of this double-edged criticism, his own radical
dissociation appears as principled action, a fighter's defiance
against continued bad faith in an industry where higher motives
should prevail. Or is it frustration *in extremis*, exemplified in a
belligerent, reckless and potentially ruinous act? Mo throwing a
tantrum because he did not get what he wanted? Or a pre-pub-
licity stunt which backfired? And has he now stepped beyond
the pale, a rogue element, shunning and shunned by the circuits
of editing, promotion and distribution in a sophisticated and
globalised industry? Reviewers have blamed idiomatic mishaps
in *Brownout* on inattentive copy-editing,[4] and in a Channel Four
'short', Mo was shown taking copies of his novel to London
booksellers, and even putting them on the shelves himself.[5]
Beyond the literary-critical brief of this book, the *Brownout*
incident might be explored as a Cultural Studies case study on
the crisis of the writer in the marketplace, or, as a counterpoint
to Salman Rushdie and *The Satanic Verses* controversy, on the
writer's contest for creative autonomy in the public sphere.[6]

The shifts in Mo's narrative strategies from earlier novels
are a much more subtle matter than the publication controversy,
but one with just as many and unfathomable possible consequences. In the reviews, the focus on the excremental Prologue
tends to overshadow the rest of the novel. It is as if the reviewers,
like some of the publishers – if reports are to be believed – could
not manage to get beyond the complex of shock, fascination and
revulsion generated by the skilfully-detailed and scatological
subject matter of the first nine pages of this 286-page novel. The
focus is misplaced, but not entirely mistaken, for in separating
the Prologue from the rest of the novel, it inadvertently draws
attention to the episodic and loosely constructed nature of the
narrative itself, especially in the tenuous connections between

the first and second parts. Unlike the other novels, and radically departing from the fictional autobiography in *Redundancy*, *Brownout* has no protagonist figures. The *picaro* function, which we have seen in a number of the other novels, is not embodied in any character; instead, it is assumed by the third-person narrator who roams from one group of characters and geographical location to another, subjecting each in turn to satiric scrutiny, tentatively threading connections among them, without, however, enacting intricate plot complications or enabling relations between characters to develop beyond the merely transitory.

Set in the Philippines, the novel is divided into two parts bracketed by Prologue and Epilogue. The Prologue describes a sexual encounter between a German professor, Detlef Pfeidwengeler, and a Filipina prostitute in which, among other graphic details, he climaxes as she defecates on him. The first part focuses on Filipino characters, and comprises nine chapters interspersing vignettes of the two families, the Boyets and the Inits, both living in the fictional provincial city, Gobernador de Leon. Boyet Dinolan is a corporate lawyer with the Evergreen company whose business is illegal logging and the export of rare timber. Married with two children, he lives the life of the provincial middle class, a typical, university-educated *pinoy* with literary pretensions which find satisfaction in his column, 'Up, Periscope', for a regional newspaper, *Citizen*. His closest friends work for the newspaper: the worldly-wise editor Nestor Chavez whom Boyet looks up to and with whom he forges a masculine camaraderie over repeated visits to the local brothel, and the woman journalist Jingkee Zamora. In himself, Boyet is not a very complex or imaginative character; through his very ordinariness and that of his life, Mo narrates quotidian 'Filipino' realities, and charts the different spaces of his fictional location: family, office, bar and brothel. The satiric edge which distinguishes Adolph Ng is entirely missing from Boyet; nor does he have the ingenuity of Wallace or the vivacity of Lily Chen or the intellectual seriousness of Gideon Chase.

Boyet's 'Philippines' is comfortable, if parochial, rather than the habitat of the impoverished and the exploited;[7] this has to do with his own place, one which is self-assigned as much as it is allocated to him. In the context of talking about the Philippines's colonial past and corrupt present, the novel says: 'Boyet's part in all this was that of Greek chorus, free in his commentary but as powerless against the unrolling circumstances as the protagonists' (17). Boyet's belief – embedded in the narrator's third-person observation – that he could be 'free in his commentary' is shown in the novel to be a small but telling instance of his personal vanity. The gulf between his self-image, especially as an outspoken and unintimidated journalist, and the cautious tones of his column speaks of a life of compromise which, in his frequent betrayals of his wife, further becomes mean and tawdry. In Boyet, Mo fashions a disempowered social subject, helpless against history and the corruption of his present circumstance. But Boyet is hardly a victim, in the sense that his insignificance is not framed by political oppression or economic exploitation. In the novel, it is his vain self-delusion which pushes him to the edge of his family and community, and eventually to the edge of the field of potential that is his own life. Boyet is pedestrian and the satirist's optic focuses on the venality in his ordinariness. Besides Boyet, none of the other characters in his social milieu is given much narrative attention, and as a result, provincial 'Filipino' society comes across as a fortuitous gathering of characters in everyday social encounters rather than a place of strong communal bonds.[8]

Much further up in the provincial hierarchy than the Boyets stand Congressman Init and his wife, Victoria, politicians and patrons of most of the business deals in Gobernador de Leon from which they garner substantial personal profits. He is humourless, corrupt, and lecherous, and is hardly more than a caricature, though an extremely comical one. While 'his essential menace [resided] in his stolid ordinariness', 'she had charisma' and 'again, unlike her Mister, she was not frightened to delegate' (196). She looks upon her marriage as a quasi-political alliance in which her husband, whom she addresses as 'Congressman', becomes the channel for her ambition while she gratifies him with her consummate skills as hostess, consort and counsel. 'She is an energiser' (196) – 'Init' means hot, as Mo is to tell us in *Renegade or Halo*[29] – the binary opposite of the phlegmatic Boyet, another variation on Lily Chen, just as single-minded and unembarrassed by self-doubt, moved by sentiment but much more completely immune than Lily to finer feelings of love and affection. Her only truth, unselfconsciously assumed, is fealty to her own interests; and as with Lily, Mo both admires and diminishes Mrs Init. His affection for these two women characters speaks of true insight into their essential self-sufficiency and their cultural predicament, hamstrung by husbands far inferior to themselves. And for both women, self-realisation is coterminous with their husband's death. But in his mockery of them, Mo also shows that he has no illusions about the ruthlessness they are capable of once their will is unleashed. Consistent with his cynicism about the 'heroic', Mo does not connect the women's transformation with social agency; their personal lives may change for the better, but their energies are expended on securing a slice of the world, not on reforming it.

Through Boyet and Mrs Init, Mo offers a profile of 'Philippines' society; we are meant to construe them as unexceptional, each a representative of their class in a society where good humour and easy cordiality draw a veil over systemic dysfunction. This dysfunction is captured symbolically in the 'brownouts', the Filipino slang for power failures which cause electric lights to fade to a sallow haze. In the tenuous connection between the characters, some of the underlying social problems become momentarily visible. For instance, Boyet and Mrs Init's paths cross when he writes what he considers an ironic column on her appearance at an official ceremony; she remembers the article – without registering the irony – and reminds him of it when they meet briefly at the conference opening in the second part of the novel. Already half-hearted in his initial attempt to maintain some kind of 'objective' journalistic distance, Boyet soon succumbs to Mrs Init's patronage, and becomes another of her minions. A further and more intricate plot line develops when Mrs Init's nephew, the local hoodlum, Crescente Koyaw, runs down Jingkee's daughter in a speedboat, but goes unpunished.

Boyet and the other journalists can only watch helplessly as Crescente apparently commits murder and speeds away. Even when his identity becomes known to them, they remain impotent in their anger. We see an omniscient and satiric point of view deployed on a small-town network: civility without civic responsibility, and the patronage and violence which substitute for and corrupt social relations. We also see brilliantly executed tableaux of characters and manners which derive in no small measure from Mo's ability to capture the accents, idioms and code-mixing of Filipino English in dialogue and free indirect speech. He observes oddities and quiddities rather than probes causes and motives; the novel is interested neither in analysis of the systemic exploitation which subjects poor to rich and women to men, nor in bonds of community and resistance which might have flourished locally.[10]

Though by no means heroic or psychologically profound, the Filipino characters are shown to be far more in touch with their humanity than the visiting academic and conference participants in Part Two of the novel, which spans Chapters Ten to Seventeen. Sponsored by Mrs Init, the conference is the opening event of the new convention centre of Gobernador de Leon, the monument to her ambition as the city's moderniser. In the second part, the natives are all but invisible at the conference; Boyet and a local professor, Benitez, have minor speaking roles, and Jingkee returns very briefly near the end. Rather than a linear development, the two parts of the novel can be seen as a dialogue of antithetical terms: local versus foreign, quotidian reality versus the rarefied and artificial environment of an academic conference. In these antitheses, Mo complicates his fictional discourse on 'Filipino' society, a discourse in which he eschews identification with either native (or insider) or outsider perceptions, and shows himself to be a harsh critic of both. If Part One shows Gobernador de Leon as a kind of murky and sluggish pond, the conference in Part Two is a veritable ship of fools and rogues. The metaphors I have chosen point not only to the discrepancy between the two parts but also their continuities – pond/ship – for Mo orchestrates the native and the foreign into a critique of the contemporary condition that shows their inter-penetration. On one level, the conference is the meeting point between Mrs Init's grandiose ambition to launch her backwater city into international recognition, and the monstrous egos of some of the so-called international community of academics and cultural workers. More than just a meeting place of the vainglorious, the conference is the fictional space in which the worst aspects of globalism circulate and manifest their dominance over the lives of individuals, local or foreign alike.

In representing the conferees from different parts of Asia and the west, Mo plays gleefully upon national stereotypes, and furthermore embodies in them positions on the political spectrum from extreme right to left. In a further play between character and caricature, Mo invents a register and rhetoric appropriate to each of the participants. The use of caricature is partly justified in the explanation that the participants are deliberately chosen by Carla Giotti, the professional organiser employed by Mrs Init, to reflect the supposed diversity of views on the Third World and development. Such tokenism is a measure of the superficiality of the conference which, in turn, reflects back on Mrs Init's starstruck desire for recognition rather than serious intellectual or social commitment. Mrs Init is the only native to be given prominence among the international pantheon, as if the text wishes to suggest that she and she alone has the 'sterling' qualities more than equal to those of her visitors. It can certainly be said that she and they deserve each other.

A brief list of the characters will give some sense of the mix of jovial and sarcastic humour in Mo's characterisation and caricature. Professor Pfeidwengeler reappears as a fascist sympathiser, and a supporter of the most extreme right-wing positions on race, politics and the environment. He is given ample opportunity in the text to air his revolting views, though there is no question that Mo also subjects him to merciless ridicule through a classic satirist's attack on his body: his pathetic sexuality, boils on his legs, and in the scene when he is unable to extricate the lower half of his body from the entrance to a cave and is totally exposed to the others' derisive laughter

(Chapter Sixteen). But interestingly, Mo refuses to make the professor the villain and pariah in the way the other conferees see him. He draws a clear distinction between Pfeidwengeler's right to hold and speak his views, and the historical outcome in Nazism which these views have led to, for which Pfeidwengeler cannot be held responsible. Pfeidwengeler is no hypocrite, and his rejection by the others means that his beliefs, no matter how abhorrent, are contained in rhetoric and have no issue in social action; in Mo's ironical logic, he is marginalised for expounding what he believes in, and his marginality guarantees his utterance.

No such consideration is shown to Dr Ruth Neumark, Pfeidwengeler's mighty opposite, whom Mo fashions as an ego-maniac *poseuse,* variously called a 'shrewd Jewish granny' and 'this formidable hybrid' (152). Originally South African, she has managed to develop a cult following in the west less on the basis of her autobiographies about growing up under apartheid than for her ability to spout fashionable left-wing causes and nurture a pristine media image. Mo takes every opportunity of her appearance in the novel to drive home the unsavouriness of her position as someone who claims radical credentials and the moral upper ground, and yet lives a life of First World privilege carefully concealed from the poor and oppressed with whom she professes solidarity. Mo is unsparing of her, as he is of the Libyan Omar Hamid, a career radical, whose favourite utterance is 'Of course, the English are *so* racist', a statement which the narrator describes as his 'password' to Third World solidarity, 'almost entirely blanched of emotive content' (170). A long-term client of Dr Neumark, he goes through the conference increasingly fearful of being displaced from her attention as she seeks younger and more useful 'comrades' like Rod Kienzler, a sneering Englishman who works in the media. Kienzler's complete insensitivity to others and to the Filipino environment is reiterated in the novel. Mo combines in these characters the traditional targets of the satirist: egotism, hypocrisy, and the exploitation of human sympathy and credulity for private gain and public praise. That he associates these qualities with left-wing political positions is a point to which I will return later on.

Of the lesser lights in the conference, Mo is caustic but less scornful. For instance, Gracie Hipkin, an American environmentalist, 'big as a beached whale', whose 'extreme stoutness' invokes unfortunate comparisons with what she tries to protect (153). She is a version of the ugly feminist stereotype, though Mo also shows that she is naive both about herself and others rather than actively malign. As the novel unfolds, some of the other national stereotypes attain varying measures of individuality. These include the Australian professor, Jack Beaufort, who is married to a Filipina from the countryside, and who specialises in the New Literatures in English; John Hawkins, journalist and Carla Giotti's friend, who goes on to betray her to Mrs Init; Kamla Mishra and N. S. Kumar, both from India, the former another ill-favoured left-wing feminist who quickly gravitates to Dr Neumark's orbit, and the latter urbane if rather inane; and the three Japanese, Dr Enoeda, an expert on volcanic activity, Tomoko Adachi, a Professor of English Literature who does not appear to speak any English, and whose expertise turns out to be on the Gawain poet, and Hanabishi, translator with an eye on the main chance. Chinese ethnicity returns in the shape of the farcically named B. K. Napoleon Wong, a dissident who has been imprisoned by both nationalist and communist governments, and who shifts indecisively between attacks on authoritarianism and vigorous defence of 'Asian values'.

To list these characters here is to duplicate and underline the narrative strategy in the second part: for most of the time, they are on parade, as the third-person narrative scrutinises and doubles back on each of them and their interaction, occasionally in dialogue with their observations on each other, friend or foe. Because of this strategy, the second part appears even more desultory than the first, although it can be said to mimic the organisation, pace and rhythm of large academic conferences, with their tendency to fragment into core and special interest groups and small networks. What is common to most of the foreign characters is that 'no one seemed to know much about the country they were in' (192) except as the destination at the end of a plane journey, and a post-conference pleasure-ground of bars and beaches. This crucial observation enables Mo to extract strategic and satiric advantage out of what appears to be a disjointed narrative: it justifies the sidelining of the native characters we have seen in the first part, and exposes the gulf between the participants' rhetoric of Third World solidarity and their actual perceptions. As with the first part, Mo demonstrates his consummate skills in the languages of different discourse situations. This is most evident in the forum on 'Asian Values' (Chapter Fifteen) in which he mimics the formal conference rhetoric and counterpoints it with the rambling and incoherent views of the speakers. On another occasion, the outing in Chapter Sixteen mentioned earlier on, Mo gives a virtuoso display of verbal slapstick in the farcical set piece where Professor Adachi, 'jumping up and down on his bandy, bowed legs, both feet leaving the ground simultaneously – began to beat Pfeidwengeler on his backside' (251) as the latter's 'elephantine buttocks' emerge from the cave (250). This is a good deal more invigorating, though perhaps less subtle, than the cave excursion in *A Passage to India* which it alarmingly recalls.

A final point to be made about the structure of the narrative concerns the Epilogue, in which we move forward in time to twenty-seven years after the conference, to look briefly at the outcome of the different characters. This strategy may recall the final moments of Evelyn Waugh's *Scoop*, or more pointedly of Dickens's *Hard Times* which, in its tale and critique of another city on the edge of modernity, is one literary precursor and intertext of *Brownout*. We have already seen how Mo builds into his characterisation an implicit scale of censure, and the Epilogue shows him clearly in the role of the satirist-as-moralist as he metes out poetic justice on the characters. While Boyet is made redundant by the new owners of *Citizen*, and becomes a rather seedy middle-aged man living off his wife's earnings, Jingkee Zamora is promoted to editor, and her daughter awakens from her coma. But in the fallen world of the satirist, justice does not necessarily operate; this is evident in Kienzler's irresistible rise in the media world and his eventual ennoblement. Most of the other characters continue to live largely blameless lives defined by the small compromises they strike with themselves and others. In this, Mo shows how he also understands the daily self-delusions necessary for individual sanity and sociality, and ridicules rather than condemns those who achieve a measure of personal fulfilment as a result, or manage to contain their own faults within their own immediate lives. The worst fate, that of being 'in part, eaten ... [and] later voided' (277) by a cannibalistic African dictator – this time reminiscent of Waugh's *Black Mischief* – he reserves for Omar Hamid; and the best – though no less bizarre – for Mrs Init, who becomes a United Nations specialist on technology transfer and copyright. In another twist of the satirist's knife, Dr Neumark, who first won fame through her memoirs, is struck down with Alzheimer's disease.

In the hierarchy of value Mo imposes on the human condition, his association of the worst of its frailties with left-wing positions, and the particularly nasty fate of both Omar Hamid and Dr Neumark, not only fly in the face of political correctness but provocatively overturn the positive value of ethnicity, marginality and victimhood central to postcolonial literary and cultural discourses.[11] Satire respects no national or ethnic boundaries; no political or cultural agenda, no matter how passionately argued or historically well-justified, can escape from the perils of the human condition which are the purview of the satirist. *Brownout* implicitly pitches this argument from artistic convention – which has its own ethical logic – against the inflection of art by the struggles of a radical politics increasingly manifest in late twentieth-century cultural productions and criticism. The novel strenuously disengages itself from the dominant paradigm, in order, paradoxically, to reassert fiction's commitment to social criticism by targeting all those who disable and betray sociality, irrespective of their ethnicity, gender and class. Along the way, Mo shows himself to be no respecter of pieties, postcolonial or otherwise.

Redundancy had reinstated and reasserted marginality as crisis, the fatal entrapment of individuals and societies in a history which disempowers them, and against which they can hardly resist. *Brownout* is the logical complement to *Redundancy* for its explosion of the claims of marginality in a game of power. In his highly individualistic conduct of the politics of fiction, Mo runs the serious risk of marginalising himself and his work, of being disparaged, dismissed, or simply ignored. The continuities between Mo's fictional and cultural politics are clearly visible: has he not done precisely the same in his fight with the publishers over *Brownout*, pushing himself to the extreme edge in order to win back some advantage in a fight between unequals? It can be argued that the novel and his actions over its publication witness a double-pronged attack on the abuses of marginality in two separate but also related spheres: as established paradigm in art and its criticism, and in the publication industry where it is often packaged as marketing strategy.

I return now to discussion of the novel, and its satire on the contemporary condition. The novel's epigraph on the title-page is a quotation from a UN resolution: ' "When a society is cohesive, law-abiding and productive, the source of its strength can invariably be traced to the strength of its families", UN General Assembly Resolution, December 8 1989.' What the narrative proceeds to show is precisely the opposite: the absence of cohesion and respect for the law, and the accumulation of wealth and power by the corrupt in a way which only the very cynical could describe as 'productive'. It offers glimpses of family bonds – in the Boyets and the relationship between Jingkee and her comatose daughter – that are threatened and made increasingly redundant amidst the common decadence. As an observation of general truth, the UN statement points in one direction towards empirical evidence or justification in historical reality, but it also points in another direction, towards the future, a brave new society – 'when' it happens. The novel, however, narrates the present, 'in the moral brownout that was the totality of society' (185) as seen by Boyet. In the fictional encounter between 'world' and 'home', the globalised rhetoric of the United Nations stands as a memorial to achievement and potential, while the local realities of provincial 'Philippines' mock its evasiveness and sentimentality.

In many ways, encounter is a keyword to an understanding of the novel. *Brownout* is a narrative of encounters – between people, nations, cultures; as such, its ostensible subject matter and subliminal thematics underline what is short term, expedient and incohesive in human relations. It is precisely these characteristics of encounter which the novel sees as endemic to contemporary relations, not only within national societies, but also in the increasing cultural traffic between nations. The metonymic space of such encounters is the airport, and Part Two of *Brownout* opens with a chapter that takes place literally in the transit lounge. The analogous space in local geography, which we also see in the novel, is the convention centre, a landmark of a society's transition from traditional life to modernity, or a short-term meeting place between home-world and international-world. In the nature of encounters, collisions frequently occur, and the novel tempers its sharp satiric edge with comic vignettes on cultural misunderstanding or mistranslation which paradoxically become occasions when characters achieve momentary insight into each others' motives. Collisions can also be violent and explosive, and the encounters within the Philippines or between its nationals and tourists, though often transient and non-affective, can leave scars on individuals, families and places. Mo discloses the inequities submerged beneath the ponderous UN rhetoric of globalism, and questions the possibilities of intra-national and inter-national relations free from the exploitation of the poor by the rich, the disempowered by the powerful, the meek by the violent, the quiet by the loud.

In *Redundancy*, we have already seen how multinational media corporations can make Danu appear and disappear at will from the attention of the world, and how Danu's global presence is calculable in terms of 'sound-bites' no longer than the length of the UN quotation. In another critique of globalism, Danu's struggle for independence is shown to be inevitably framed by the business interests of trans-national oil companies.[12] *Brownout* complements these insights by focusing on cultural exchanges in a supposedly globalised world, and underlines the asymmetry when such exchanges take place under the aegis of 'development', another crucial term in the UN-mediated understanding of international relations codified in the division between the economically prosperous and industrially advanced countries – the so-called 'First World' – and the poverty and privation of countries in the so-called 'Third World'.[13] In drawing attention to the material basis of cultural exchange, *Brownout* shows what 'development' means for a country like the Philippines as it joins the scramble – or 'progress' – out of the Third into the First World. Here, the satirist's optic turns to the physical and architectural transformation of the landscape and what it signifies:

> Cebu wore its best face for the Inits. Going down Jones – never mind it was named Osmeña, it would always be Jones for Victoria – she was startled by the size and quality of the up-town commercial buildings: the sawn-off replica of the Hong Kong Connaught Tower, that gross colander, Asia's tallest building not so long ago, complete here with ground-floor MacDonald's; the mighty copper-coloured Metrobank Plaza, home of equally mighty Atlas mining, detailed down to windstocking and heli-pad on roof; the Babylonic Midtown Hotel, ascending like a series of stepped glass cubes. She'd been impressed, and like her to do so [sic], registered it without qualification, the Congressman rather more grudgingly. Downtown, the megastores apart, had still been a noisome den – Colon, nation's most ancient street, the aptly named, the filthy, its drains choked in garbage, still flooding to waist height at the smallest provocation. But it all only served as a massive material counter-point to emphasise that great, that glitzy development of Cebu Uptown. (127)

Within the nation, the inequities of development are inscribed in the landscape between the rise of 'Uptown', and the decay of 'Downtown'. This spatial difference registers the mutation of colonialism which links the nation inextricably with what lies beyond it; 'Colon' is the Spanish form of Columbus (also an intestine), the inaugurating imperialist, and the pathway to evacuation – colonialism from top to bottom. The name of the country's most ancient street speaks of an historical phase of imperial conquest and government by a foreign power which has now been displaced – and replaced – by the economic and cultural invasion of 'MacDonald's'. Thus 'development' ironically means continued economic subjugation of the nation, and its recolonisation by multinational corporations, although the subtextual continuities between past and present are lost on Mrs Init as she is seduced (one might say innocently seduced) by those glossy monuments to the power of capital. Through the eyes of Mrs Init, the narrative registers the architectural fantasies of the Third World, but the satirist laughs at them as colonial imitations, like the building which looks like a 'sawn-off replica of the Hong Kong Connaught Tower' – itself a 'gross colander' – twice removed from modernist origins in the west. Rather than progress, a movement away from the past, the nation is the site of imitation, replicating not only its own history of colonisation but the histories of development elsewhere. Globalisation is the incorporation of nations into the imitation and replication of the developed world, and the sale of the past 'development' of the First World as the corporate future of the Third. In a similar way, as Mo sees it, the Third World invites the First to feed off it discursively, in the conference supposed to testify to 'development'.

The novel reiterates this point in its satire on the architecture of 'Filipino' progress: Manila airport, 'a monument to inappropriateness, to profligate folly and grandiosity' where 'such natural light as there was filtered through smoked glass of bullet-proof specification' and 'the air was stale and still' because frequent brownouts disrupt the air-conditioning (140). The convention centre in Gobernador de Leon reproduces Mrs Init's fond memories of a visit to Italy; fully computerised, with 'air-con capable of cutting to the bone', and a 'p/a system [that] was karaoke class' (158), the end result is a 'post-modernist Sistine chapel' (168). These visible follies of 'progress' have more sinister undersides that are shielded from the public eye. Evergreen, Boyet's employer, evolves from a national corporation involved in illegal logging to the shipment of toxic wastes from Germany to the Philippines, thus colluding in making the nation a dumping ground for the First World, and incidentally repeating the scene of the Prologue on a larger scale. In a cameo reappearance, three of the triads from *Sour Sweet* turn up to discuss with Mrs Init investment in her city, driving a hard bargain whereby they can launder the proceeds of drug trafficking. The encounters of the local with the global, which guarantee 'development' in the Third World, link up native with international corruption in a 'moral brownout' that envelops not only individual societies but defeats 'society' as the principle and organisation of collective human existence. Third World becomes 'Turd World', in the novel's irrepressible scatology. Executing poetic justice, the novel develops its own radical solutions. The convention centre is wrecked by grenades, and Congressman Init gunned down by his political enemies. In a parallel act of sabotage which is also revenge against Mrs Init, Carla introduces a virus into the computer files of the conference, destroying all records of its proceedings. Wrapped in comic guise, the novel condemns the contemporary society it has satirised to quasi-apocalyptical punishment, and deletes it. It justifies its own vindictiveness, however, by showing that fire and disease happen not because of divine retribution, but as the implosion of a society no longer able to sustain the burden of 'development', like an overloaded electricity generator emitting sparks and flames as it collapses into a final 'brownout'.

In a literary career which inclines with increasing steepness away from the axes of market and academe, *Brownout*, which signals fundamental change, is also a calculated risk for Mo. On one level, the capacity for risk is the will to experiment, and Mo declares that what he values most in a writer 'is self-renewal through different creations'. 'I do not like writers who continually repeat themselves,' he adds,

> who write novels which look the same, with the same characters, the same settings, even in the same tone. Although a lot of writers spend their lives like that, I cannot accept the monotony of plucking old creative strings. I would rather write six or seven different books than sixteen similar ones. In my own writing, I try my

best to change, to create what's new. I could have written more books in the past fifteen years, but I have chosen every time to break new paths instead.[14]

It is precisely this experimenting will which drives Mo further and further away towards the edges and precipices of cultures and societies in his choice of subject matter, to venture into terrain made inhospitable by the lack of sympathetic attention, and to re-present them to the world through his fiction. But in his seemingly limitless ability to antagonise and outrage, Mo could alienate precisely those whose sympathies he wishes to engage – if not for himself, at least for those subjects whose lives and predicament inspire his satiric art. Resolutely individualist, Mo has so far been extremely astute in judging how far he can take his individualism while retaining a large measure of collective endorsement in both critical esteem and popular reception of his novels. Whether that judgement will continue to counterbalance the fascination of risk is crucial to the future shape of Mo's career.

Renegade or Halo²:
a postscript

RENEGADE or Halo² capitalises on some of Mo's strengths in narrative and, true to his spirit of adventure, attempts to push back once again the frontiers of his subject matter. Tackling a fresh subject matter with characteristic passion, Mo, in Renegade or Halo² offers both familiar patterns and a renewed satiric drive. The dilatoriness which haunts Brownout continues to shadow Renegade or Halo², but is more consistently offset by dramatisations of character and their circumstances. In the person of Rey Castro, the first-person narrator of Renegade or Halo², Mo has identified and crafted a subject who can perform credibly the ambitious task of narrating the world at the end of the twentieth century. Told by Castro, offspring of an African–American serviceman and a Filipina bar-girl, the novel captures some of the brilliance of the first-person narrative in The Redundancy of Courage. Castro's many voices speak of a complex interiority unavailable to Boyet Dinolan, and in him, the picaro function finds its most contemporary embodiment as an illegal migrant worker. After the hesitation of Brownout, it appears that Mo has retrenched, at least for his latest novel to date, in the groove of his unique abilities.

While Brownout on Breadfruit Boulevard resonates with comic laughter at the less salubrious aspects of Filipino society, Renegade or Halo² shows a much stronger sense of affectionate disenchantment with the country and its institutionalised corruptions. The time, it seems, has come for another departure. In a move which recalls the dislocations of the Chinese family, and the epical turn to nineteenth-century China, *Renegade or Halo²* begins in the Philippines but moves across a multitude of societies and cultures; its horizons are the world at the close of the century. Castro grows up in the Philippines where he receives a Jesuit education and is poised to advance socially through legal training at university when he becomes involved in a brutal fight between opposing fraternities, and takes the blame for murder. Fleeing the Philippines, he becomes a stowaway and watches as his friends are murdered on board ship by the Ukrainian crew. He joins the global underclass of illegal workers, migrating through Hong Kong, the Gulf, England and Cuba, before ending back where he started in the Philippines.

Taking off from the picaresque tradition, Mo pushes hard in one direction at his own artistry, and in another at the boundaries externally imposed upon individuals by circumstances of birth, cultural tradition and the nation-state. *Halo²*, pronounced 'Hallow-Hallow' (231), a very sweet concoction of coloured syrup, shaved ice, beans and diced coconut, mixes colours and flavours, the solid and the liquid; it is eaten and drunk as dessert but is as filling as a meal, and local ingredients are added in as the basic concoction is remixed in various parts of Southeast Asia. Its choice as a tag in the novel's title is typically Mo: a clever dash of the local transformed symbolically so as to take on transcultural meaning, and particularly appropriate to the provenance and story of the protagonist-narrator. As Castro himself explains, '*Halo²* is a whole bunch of ingredients that shouldn't belong together but work when you combine them' (232). But like Mo's other rather cumbersome titles, *The Redundancy of Courage* and *Brownout on Breadfruit Boulevard*, it is awkward and hence, teasing.

In the novel, Mo exploits the strengths in sustained first-person narrative which we saw, for the first time, in *The Redundancy of Courage*. Hybrid in himself, Castro's voice takes on the tones and nuances of the culturally unbound. As the voice of the Filipino in the world, it suggests an open and easy-going nature; it invites companionship, both male and female, which helps to smooth Castro's passage through his many trials.

Part of Castro's charm for the reader is his ability to translate the serious and high-minded into the earthy and profane. The epigraph of the novel, '*el demonico de las compariciones*', is taken from the writing of José Rizal, Filipino independence fighter and national hero. Castro observes, 'Rizal ... wrote of ... the restlessness and uncertainty brought on by too wide a knowledge of the world. The indigestion *halo-halo* can bring on, I guess' (29). The irreverence is typical, and in this brief observation, Castro displays a mental facility for shifting from other to self, high to low, the serious to the comic. Geniality is also a necessary virtue for someone like Castro, born without a stake in society. Heard in dialogue, his public voice is sensitively attuned to the myriad linguistic changes of diverse interlocutors. In virtuoso performances of his auditory talent, Mo represents and mimics the varieties of English used in both spoken and written forms by his global cast of characters. English speaks with many tongues in the narrative, and Castro's own voice, which articulates the idioms and idiosyncrasies of Filipino English, is serially inflected so as to accommodate and, in stringent circumstances, to adapt to shifts in verbal and social codes. Like Adolph Ng, Castro is a survivor; while enjoying better fortune than his fellow scapegoated friends and itinerants, an undoubted strategy of his survival is the ability to bond with his exploiters, to assume the manner of subservience and nurture their reliance on his indispensable service. In doing so, he exercises but also masks an intelligence that is no less muscular than the physique with which he is endowed.

This intelligence is audible only to the novel's readers through Castro's other or inner voice which performs the fictional tasks of observation, narration, reflection and commentary. It is also the voice which distinguishes him from 'the respectful, place-knowing poor' (49), like his mother and aunties, who remain content in their privation. Necessarily double-voiced, Castro engages the readers by offering them privileged insight into his duplicity. In contrast to his easy-going and pliable outward self, the inner voice is opinionated and often insightful, and shifts across a number of comic registers: the wry, amused aside, the self-deprecating joke, the mocking insinuation and sly civility, the scabrous or scatological thrust. It speaks of a highly developed self-consciousness, and creates the space in the novel for Castro as agent and free-thinking subject. By counter-pointing the two voices of the obliging subordinate in company and the shrewd observer in private, the novel keeps in focus a constant irony. The distance between the two voices reveals Castro's ability to deflect, elude and rise above the monologic discourses of his exploiters; its enactment is the novel's political message. The novel refuses to make him a victim, and refuses to allow the reader to think of him as one. At the same time, exile and unbelonging, violence and exploitation are graphically depicted through his narration, and leave no question as to the authorial censure of the conditions in which Castro and his fellow members of the global underclass are forced to live.

But in revealing his thoughts, Castro also reveals his short-comings and complicity.[1] For instance, though undeceived by the venality of the spoilt rich boys of the Filipino legal fraternity and their sinister patron, the lawyer Atty Caladong, he has few qualms about ingratiating himself with them. There are also significant tonal differences between Adolph Ng's and Castro's voices. Mo has said that he dislikes Ng, whom he describes as a 'rat'.[2] Ng's unheroic squealing and whimpering stands in contrast to Castro's even tenor which speaks recurrently of composure under duress. But it is precisely this composure that is unsettling. A striking example can be seen in the nightmarish scene where a Filipina, Haydee, whom Castro knows and likes, is gang-raped and then stabbed to death by the fraternity boys in a drug-induced frenzy. A witness to Haydee's torture, Castro describes the repeated beating in clinical detail. After her death, at the urging of the gang intent on distributing their guilt, he takes up the knife offered to him and adds his own stab-wound to the dead body. But he narrates this extra horror dispassion-ately, anti-climatically: 'I took the knife from Skip and did it. There was no more resistance or drama than there would have been stabbing a foam-cushion' (113). Shortly after, when they set out to dispose of the body, he is told to drive:

> I said nothing and got in. We are powerless against some
> imperatives, even though we may be fully conscious of
> them. This was a cultural imperative, man: to keep my
> trap shut and my face blank, even though I thought the
> seating arrangements were what Butch would have chosen
> on his blackboard as the best to mark me and Dant, to pop
> us with head-shots without warning, to neutralise my
> dangerous hands. (114)

Here is a moment when a full consciousness of his situation
makes Castro's quiescence much more culpable. But more importantly, what is the substance of this consciousness? If we look
at the passage closely in its context, it raises far more questions
about Castro than it answers. What is the 'cultural imperative'
he speaks of? Is it the law of the tribe, or the unspoken code of
fraternal bonding which he cannot break without destroying his
own identity and belonging? (There are plenty of references to
'tribes' and the 'tribal' before this moment and throughout the
novel, and this is a significant thematic which I will return to
later on.) Does his uncomplaining obedience spring from a class
habit or a macho code? Or is this reference to 'cultural imperative' an unconscious rationalisation of his complicity in the
act of murder? Another possibility is that he is not so much
concerned about the murder as about the fact that he is not
trusted by the gang, and therefore must gain that trust by
keeping his 'trap shut' and 'face blank'. He is alternately 'powerless', and a man with 'dangerous hands', that is to say, one who
has the potential of turning the tables on those who disempower
him. Is the former his self-perception, and the latter a matter of
what others see and fear in him? And is he registering the
contradiction between the two in order to reveal the gap between
what he is and how he appears to the world? If he does believe he
has 'dangerous hands', then what is he saying about his acts of
submission to Skip? At a confessional moment after an extreme
crisis, Castro's inner voice seems to offer a transparent self-
evaluation, but it is not a telling voice, and in the vast gap of
what it does or does not manage to say, the focus on Castro is
strangely blurred.

Mo seems to have prepared for this possibility from the very beginning of the novel – or perhaps this is an instance of what playing to his own strength as novelist means. Reflecting upon his classical education under the Jesuits, Castro says: 'I didn't kid myself, man. Father Paul's great gift to me was the ability to be dispassionate about myself, to see things cold-eyed from the outside... What he gave me, Castro the sneak, the wind-up dinosaur, was a cool heart and a permanent emancipation from tribalism' (32–3). Being 'dispassionate', 'cold-eyed', and 'cool' about the self may well be virtues – and Castro clearly seems to think so – but in relations between the self and others, they can become the code-words of an emotional dereliction that issues in failed sociality. In his eyewitness account of Haydee's rape and murder, Castro gives a virtuoso performance of self-detachment that is followed through, first in his participation in the disposal of the body and then in his restrained self-reflection. Though resolutely un-'tribal' in withholding sympathy from Haydee, he is far less able to remain 'emancipated' from the tribal pressures of the fraternity; in the latter case, being 'dispassionate' and 'cool' is clearly not enough to ensure his self-determination and autonomy.

After his short reflection, Castro never once returns to his own role in the tragedy of Haydee's death, and more importantly, it has little demonstrable effect on him. It is the same with the rape and murder of his best friend, Danton, on board the ship where they stowed away: another particularly violent episode in the novel. Castro avenges Danton's death before he jumps ship, and conjures his friend's memory from time to time as he remembers, much less frequently, the murdered Haydee. The two set-pieces on Haydee's and Danton's murders demonstrate once again Mo's forte as the novelist of violence, and may be read as indictments of the Filipino predicament, and the extreme cruelties which human beings can inflict upon one another. They do not flesh out Castro's character, or if they do, it is detrimentally, by showing how lacking in affect he is.

At issue is not whether circumstances allow Castro to act, or whether he is ethical or unethical. The critical question is that his voice is paradoxically both multivocal and under-performed. In the long term, what is not shown is the emotional and psychological impact of the two murders upon him, both as a witness and as friend. About a hundred pages on from Danton's death, Castro comments obliquely on how words distort: 'When you thought, shaped, and scribbled, you were distilling, you got essence; and it burned like witch-hazel. People you liked or loved got distorted. I mean, I'd loved Danton like the brother I didn't have, but he wouldn't have thought it from some of the observations I could have formulated about him' (234). As a general comment on the process of writing, it is insightful, but as an act of memory, it floats free of the horrifying circumstances of Danton's death. It is impossible to speculate what place his murder has on Castro's memory of their relationship, or indeed, whether it has any place at all.

It can be argued that the picaresque narrative lends itself to this under-performance. Thinking back once again to Henry Fielding's *Tom Jones*, its narrative dynamic foregrounds adventure and satire rather than psychological realism and the analysis of character. *Renegade or Halo²* is true to this literary heritage in the narrative roller-coaster that plunges Castro repeatedly into turbulent situations and encounters. As the *picaro* moves in and out of imbroglios, in *Tom Jones* and its nineteenth-century successors, the narrative pattern is enacted as a succession of episodes. The two murders in *Renegade or Halo²* that I have just referred to appear as self-complete episodes, leaving the barest trace on both the causality of the novel and the psychology of the *picaro*, Castro himself. Torture and suffering, described in their full horror, hold little terror for Castro, and analogically, his intimacies have little romance. He is as clinical in describing his love-making with Louise, a nurse he meets in Bohaiden, as he is in describing Haydee's or Danton's death. The English picaresque eschews both the gothic and the romantic, those representations of psychic and emotive forces which draw the character inwards away from the domain of observable empirical action.

But psychological realism is not incompatible with the picaresque. Becky Sharpe in *Vanity Fair* is as highly motivated by force of circumstance as her predecessor in the female picaresque, Defoe's Moll Flanders. What Becky has, in addition, is a finely-wrought sense of motive, and it is the psychological world, or mindscape, opened up in her that makes her a more fully present – if not more likeable – character than Moll, and makes the novel she is in a landmark text renewing the picaresque tradition. From Defoe and Fielding to Thackeray, the picaresque narrative has extended its compass, and the earlier episodic structure which seemed to work against character formation has turned out to be flexible enough to enable journeys into a character's inner world no less adventurous.

In this light, Castro appears both true to the *picaro* type and also under-performed. If his reactions to the horror of what he has witnessed seem muted, this is illustrative of the novel's overall restraint in probing the more profound reaches of his emotions and psyche. Listening to Castro is like listening to a raconteur of breathtaking experiences; the raconteur is skilled and perceptive, but there are few hints that he is either transformed by these experiences or in their telling. Castro's voice seldom falters in its self-consciousness, and as I have pointed out earlier on, it has an interesting variety of tones and registers. Unvaried in its variety, but without signalling an inner transformation, in the course of a novel lasting for almost five hundred pages, it becomes repetitious and palls, and its satiric edge is blunted. Meanwhile we watch more and more of the hero's experiences without really learning anything more about him.

The episodes in the latter third of novel also tend increasingly to repeat a set pattern: Castro moves on to a new society and culture, meets with people who exploit or befriend him, and comments wittily and knowingly on their foibles. While an episodic structure is characteristic of the picaresque, Coleridge, writing from outside the tradition, has astutely observed of *Tom Jones* that it has one of 'the three most perfect plots ever planned'.[3] Plot is not possible without causality. Causality in turn means the exploration of why events turn out the way they do, and central to this exploration are the motives of individuals, the twists and turns of their emotions and reasoning as they shape, and are shaped by, their own histories and the world they are in. The final outcome or *dénouement* is rendered explicable not only in terms of what happens to, but also what happens within, the characters. Castro's strength and constant interest as character comes from his ability to see himself with minimal illusion, and from Mo's consistently virtuoso performance of his narrating voice. But this is counterpointed by the barest reflection, beyond exigency, into why he acts as he does. In the absence of an historical frame like, for example, the Danuese insurgency in *The Redundancy of Courage*, what happens to Castro seems entirely a matter of accident, from the accident of his birth to the numerous unforeseen or at best loosely connected encounters that make up his story. Together with minimal change in interiority, Castro is cut loose from any structure of causality, historical or psychological. The fact that *Renegade or Halo*[2] does not invest much in causality suggests a creative disregard of convention, and might place it in the context of the contemporary post-modernist critique of causality and other protocols of realism. But this sits uneasily with the fact that the novel is very much in the realist mode. Above all, as a narrative in which one character's point of view is paramount, causality is a vital resource for change and variation, and its displacement leads to repetitiousness and a thinning and flattening of the first-person voice.

While picaresque conventions are embedded in the texture of the novel itself, the one outstanding literary predecessor which *Renegade or Halo*[2] frequently invokes is Mary Shelley's *Frankenstein*. The novel's title sounds like a parody of *Frankenstein, or the Modern Prometheus*. Specifically, the recurrent cross-references between Castro and the Creature – to whom the novel for the most part knowingly misassigns the name of Frankenstein – can be seen to replace any exploration into the further reaches of Castro's identity. The Frankenstein references do not emanate from a stable point of view. They represent the way Castro sees himself, and his perception of how he is seen by others; they can also be used as a descriptive shorthand, as in 'the Philippine Frat was a Frankenstein version of the American college fraternity' (50). As both self-representation and the perception of others, they point to Castro's physical differences from his Filipino compatriots, and the suggestions of monstrosity that shadow his identity. Inheriting his father's colour and muscular physique, Castro is very much out of place in the Philippines, and his detachment emerges, at least in part, as a survival mechanism and cultural adaptation in a society which sees him in racist terms as an alien. Entangled with the Frankenstein theme are questions of paternity, and the relations between a father-creator and his offspring. Castro never discovers who his father is, but in the course of the novel, he defines himself in relation to a number of father-figures. The Jesuit priests who are his teachers, Father Paul and Father Boy, are seen as positive father-figures to whom Castro owes not only his education, but also a mind that can work like a schoolman and pedant, and always with unyielding self-awareness and intelligence. The decency of Mr Smith, the English dentist who is his Hong Kong employer, adds another dimension to Castro's understanding of humane values. He takes shape in the binary opposition between these positive father-figures and negative ones like Atty Caladong and Faud, his Arab employer in the fictional Gulf emirate of Bohaiden. From the latter two, who are both employers and exploiters, Castro acquires knowledge of the criminal and the anti-social. Through his association with these father-figures, book-learning and a knowing and very worldly wisdom are played off against each other to produce the '*halo*[2]' of his critical intelligence.

Mary Shelley's novel is fraught with anxiety about the question of origins, caught as it was between the residual discourse of Creation and providence and its displacement by an Enlightenment discourse which put a premium on education and self-making. Frankenstein is doomed by a double transgression: in arrogating to himself the divine power of creation, and in his rejection of his progeny, which transforms the Creature into a monster. Through the Creature's first-person narrative, we see how a passion for learning and self-improvement degenerates into sociopathic fury because of social and paternal neglect and repudiation. As this degeneration occurs, the discourse of man's postlapsarian evil, subsumed so far by the novel's nature–culture debate, resurges to attempt a closure on the debate. Like *Frankenstein, Renegade or Halo*² foregrounds Castro's identity as a construct, an identity acquired after birth in part through a series of associations that mimic the father–son relationship. But Mo's novel is liberated from anxiety about created nature in that Castro spends very little time wondering about his father or that element of his composition which might be inherited. The notion of identity as a construct challenges racist perceptions predicated on given biological nature which, in Mo's novel, stigmatise Castro no matter where he goes. Empowered by his wit, and a trained and disciplined intelligence, Castro can see how others see him, through to the fear of difference which lies at the heart of their racism. As he fathoms the origins of racism, Castro also plays on this fear by manipulating the physical threat which he poses, using his size to mask his intelligence in order to fit into the brawny-but-brainless stereotype, or to maximise his advantage at moments of peril. His identity is his wit, and the novel is very clear that this is a construct of nurture and experience rather than nature.

While this wit offers Castro relief from racist oppression, it is by no means entirely blameless, and at moments, actually turns on the novel's anti-racist and anti-essentialist discourse. Castro is as quick to stereotype others, and reduce entire cultures to a convenient summary of fixed qualities. Beginning from 'home', he calls the Philippines, 'a nation which didn't even possess the collective self-discipline to form a queue for ferry-tickets' (63); 'We pinoys ... with our syrupy natures, we were the caries-creating sugar in the *Halo*²,' he adds, 'the tart Singaporeans the palate-scouring citric acids' (229–30). The Chinese, true to their legendary inscrutability, have 'empty faces' (65); a Chinese father 'would have drowned' his daughter at birth (139); Hong Kong 'wasn't just a place that was efficient, you could take that for granted with the ruthless Chinese. It was that the Chinese lack of compassion encompassed themselves as well' (143). The British, in the persons of the admired Mr Smith and his county wife, fare better; as good losers, they are not 'so much un-Asian as un-everyone, including un-American. It was quintessentially British.' But Castro adds, even-handedly, 'I didn't think it was creditable. It didn't spring from modesty but a deep, submerged arrogance that was Roman in its completeness and its nihilism, and Japanese in its hypocrisy. It wasn't Jesuitical, for sure; they were hell-bent on being winners' (139). And to round off but by no means complete this list, the Bohaidenese face is characterised by 'a semitic nose that looked it could wound, the hard and pitiless eye, the thin upper lip' (278). It is possible to argue that these statements should not be measured against some extra-textual standard of political correctness, but must be placed in the context of Castro's vantage as an often abused employee who sees people and cultures at their worst. Thus the Smiths get off the most lightly because they treat him best of all. But it is in the generalising, conscious or unconscious, from the individualised other to generic type – or from 'he/she' to 'they' – that the mechanism of racist and cultural stereotyping is set in motion.[4] In this respect, how Castro thinks, rather than what or why he thinks, underlines the crudeness of this mechanism. To argue this point is to explore one of the ways by which the text problematises the first-person narrator: how it shows in him a kind of blindness that replicates the process the world uses to stigmatise and diminish him. But it has to be said that Mo's novels without exception are never shy about offering generalised observations on nationalities, ethnicities and culture. Sometimes attributed to a particular character or narrator and sometimes not, it is a boldness entirely characteristic of this writer and has probably made him more enemies than anything else.

Related to the question of origins is that of belonging, and as a corollary to its critique of racism, Mo's novel examines the tribe and tribalism as a form of human community. If ethnicity can denote the positive values of shared tradition and communal solidarity in late twentieth-century cultural semantics, the tribe, as it is represented in Mo's novel, is its negative term. In

Castro's world, tribes are savage, the fusion of primal and barbaric human urges whipped into action by specific combinations of circumstances. In many ways, tribes are culturally bound, the performances, in ensemble, of the psychopathologies which the special circumstances of their members entail. The bonds which tie an individual to a tribe, and the compulsions which a tribe exerts upon its members, are scrutinised and satirised. Castro shows how tribes define themselves against an other, an individual or a different tribe, whom it traduces, seeks to dehumanise and ultimately to destroy. The Frats' gang-rape and murder of Haydee exemplifies this dynamic of self-definition and tribal bonding among the members; it is an act of selection by which the reluctant and faint-hearted are identified and made to endure whatever fate of exclusion awaits them. While Castro is helpless against tribal coercion at that moment, his detachment can be seen as a kind of mental prophylactic against the psychosis of the savage. He is diminished as a human being, but this is the price he has to pay to defend himself against the annihilation of all that is human in him. Castro's worldly wisdom is punctuated by many such compromises, conscious or unconscious, throughout the novel.

He remains constantly vigilant about tribal co-optation. This vigilance springs from an awareness of how seductive tribal collectivity can be to someone like him, how it can provide conduits to social advancement, protection and the security of a known place. At the same time, he is careful to distinguish tribal urges from the spontaneous identification that arises when he sees someone like himself, similarly out-of-place. These moments of identification inject a recurrent *frisson* into Castro's detachment. Thus, early in the novel, he and his friends help a Vietnamese refugee detained in a Filipino camp to escape. Another dramatic example is his encounter with a group of albinos (80–2). In colour terms, they are his radical opposites, but they also share a similar position in the Filipino ecology, at once habituated and estranged. He finds friendship and sexual gratification among the Filipina migrant domestics; to the memory of his dead friends, and those friends he makes in his migrations, he shows both a loyalty of sentiment and comradely attachment. As he says, 'I was a man, that was my primary visible tribe, but I was also underdog by birth and by temperament. That was my real tribe, that of the despised outsiders, trying to get in from the cold' (169). In this respect, Castro's tribe is culturally un-bound, a comradeship which crosses gender and race, in a global underclass whose migrancy is set in motion by the dynamics of capitalism in the late twentieth century. It is a group you do not often find getting serious attention in the pages of an English novel.

This cross-cultural discourse of solidarity is, however, only one side of the story. *Renegade or Halo²*, like all of Mo's novels, narrates the ambivalent spaces of the transgressive and the recalcitrant. Though as mentally agile as he is geographically mobile, Castro cannot but reach out for certainty and stability. His prejudices exemplify this desire in the negative, the opposite of which is his adulation of Mr Smith. In the push and pull of the narrative, this desire for the certain and the categorical is made visible and immediately questioned: 'Commander Smith's virtues, those absolutes I had been disposed to worship, I was starting to see as relatives, as part of my own Philippine family of vices. They were only successful in their own context, in a better society. Standards you could live up to in London or Seattle simply ensured your doom in Bohaiden or Manila or Bombay or Surabaya' (320). Castro's vantage is both cross-cultural and culture-bound; an ability to compare and contrast cultures undergirds the perception that virtue is not culturally transferable.

Despite the distances he has travelled across cultures, person-ally and in his fiction, Mo has remained true to those discrimin-ations which he professed at the beginning of his career. Recently, in an interview to mark the publication of *Renegade or Halo²*, he says, 'it seems to me absolutely demonstrable that cultures are different. And if they are different, they will by definition be unequal… A society where you're taken off in the middle of the night for torture, or your kids fail an exam at school because you don't pay a bribe to the teacher: they are inferior societies.'⁵ Mo's satiric humour is often sharp and wintry as he looks at characters and cultures who fail to measure up in his hierarchy of values, and he reserves a special outrage for those who traduce the values they profess to guard. What he is most concerned with, and what moves him as a novelist, is the basic right of human beings to a decent life – the security of a good night's sleep, education for one's children – rather than specific social and political causes and movements. There is an awkward compassion, that is entirely consonant with the satiric misanthropy, and issues in magnanimous laughter at human folly. It is precisely at moments of social and political upheaval that this morality requires re-articulation, and in Mo's novels, from *An Insular Possession* onwards, a rootless, shifting, and turbulent world is seen through the telescopic lens of those in the frontline who are most impacted upon and most defenceless, and therefore have the greatest need for certainty, even if this means embracing the cause of the violent and the unjust.

This is a crucial point of departure between characters and author. His characters scramble for the basic ingredients of survival and a reasonable life, for which they are prepared to compromise their sense of rightness and wrong. But for Mo, they become the unyielding demands of an outspoken morality. This morality provides him with a stable yardstick for judging people and cultures, the past and the present. He seems to be driven by a strongly-felt need to judge, and it is this need – rather than the actual substance of the moral position itself – together with his habit of publicising judgements as verbal provocations, which define his public identity as author. In his longest article so far on a non-literary subject, Mo addresses a contentious issue at the centre of pan-Asian politics. In the article, his recurrent preoccupations – political oppression and the ordeals of victims that remain largely unknown and unreported, the insidiousness of cultural relativism – are linked together in a serious indictment of Japanese atrocities against other Asian nations during the Second World War, their refusal to apologise or to compensate those who have suffered, and the collusion of the west in this continued evasion of history.⁶ The article has two points of origin. The first is the visit to Britain, two months earlier, of the Japanese Prime Minister, and the connivance of the British tabloid press in what Mo sees as the Japanese wooing of the British public. In launching his attack, Mo returns to another point of origin, to Hong Kong, where 'the brutality of the Japanese ... during the occupation is not so well known', and reports in unforgiving detail what he knows from childhood stories, visits to old battlegrounds and recent research, of the atrocities committed there. For Mo, the guilt of the Japanese is unquestionable, and is very real, measurable in statistics of deaths under internment, tortures and rapes. His speaks with an outrage, and on behalf of the victims, which counterpoints the subtle contemplation of real or imaginary guilt that was the achievement of Ishiguro's *An Artist of the Floating World* (1986).

The accounts he reports of the Japanese occupation of Hong Kong and other parts of Asia bring to mind the *malai* colonisation of Danu in *The Redundancy of Courage*, and as Mo goes on to talk about the 'unlikely heroes' of the occupation, images of Danuese resistance and its futility are refreshed with a new (and old) and all too realistic gloss. When Mo turns once more to the Japanese, this intertextual connection develops a new and lethal twist: 'Courage is a wide term covering different manifestations. Daring and fortitude are not the same thing at all. In fact, the daring tend to have no fortitude and vice versa. The preference of some Japanese soldiers in the last days of the war to be killed rather than surrender does not strike me as courageous. I find it less fanatical than nihilistic and I have always found nihilism to be a kind of cowardice.'

Throughout the article, Mo is sombre and severe and, significantly, his customary satiric tenor is missing. But the satirist's relentless pursuit of all human failure continues to drive Mo as he rounds on two forms of apology for the Japanese, the first ironically issuing from former internees who write of their experience, and achieve some kind of cathartic liberation through the process of narration. 'It is much harder', says Mo grimly, 'to carry the burden of anger all your life than it is to drop it. To say that one's tormentors were somehow different from oneself and bound by another code of ethics is to give the experience the moral neutrality of having been mauled by wild animals.' He is no less harsh on the second kind of apology:

> What makes the Japanese record between 1937 and 1945 so disgraceful is the consistent and institutionalised nature of the cruelty towards the helpless. Some Westerners seek to explain it by saying that the Japanese code of military honour decreed that a soldier die rather than surrender and that POWs had forfeited all right to be treated as humans. This is part of the post-war Western fashion for cultural relativism and it leads to a very dangerous moral double standard. Cultures certainly collide through misunderstanding – I owe my existence to such a collision – but there is also such a thing as essential evil, which is not to be mitigated by reference to context.[7]

In its vivifying narrative of history and in the tenor of its personal belief, the article has assembled all the ingredients of a Timothy Mo novel. It is also possessed by the satirist's indignation at social and political injustice and its roots in human iniquity. But for all its provocations, there is also caution in the way the article focuses on specific and documented incidents of Japanese conduct during and after the Second World War. Unlike his characters, who are quick to typify entire cultures, Mo, when speaking in his own voice resists the temptation to generalise on the Japanese and Japanese culture in such a way as to insert them into his hierarchy of world cultures. No such restraint inhibits Rey Castro's observations on the places and peoples he encounters on his odyssey.

Critical overview and conclusion

THOUGH his work is widely reviewed, there has been surprisingly little sustained critical attention to Mo's fiction – a few articles, and no full-length book until the present work. The articles tend either to focus on 'Chineseness' in Mo's early novels, or to situate him among an international pantheon of writers. In the former case, Mo's critical antagonism towards 'Chinese' culture has been given a philosophical gloss from within the culture itself,[1] while the latter approach tends to exemplify current academic interest in authors and writing which cross the overlapping boundaries of cultures, communities and nation-states. What is needed – and it is this need which the present work seeks to address – is criticism which explores the two dimensions of Mo's work in relation to each other, so that its supposed 'Chinese', 'ethnic' or 'native' preoccupations and its ambient global consciousness can be seen to interact on a number of levels: formally in the choice of subject matter, fictional locations and characterisation; thematically in constructions of identities and cultures; and in the satiric critique of the human condition in the contemporary world.

There are a number of reasons for the relative critical neglect of Mo, and chief among them is the awkward fact that a writer like him does not fit readily into existing academic categories or fields of study. Thus to discuss this critical neglect is to throw light on the limitations of academic categorisation. Here Rushdie's observations from a separate but related context are worth remembering. Complaining about the label 'Commonwealth

Literature', he says, 'the creation of a false category can and does lead to excessively narrow, and sometimes misleading readings of some of the artists it is held to include; and again, the existence – or putative existence – of the beast distracts attention from what is actually worth looking at, what is actually going on'.[2] Mo and his work call into question, as Rushdie does, received academic categories and the boundaries between them. Mo is not incorporable into Sinology because he is not mono-ethnically Chinese, and there is the question of his fictional compass which far exceeds any 'Chinese' milieu. On the other hand, ironically, as we have seen, it is precisely his Chinese ancestry which is at the crux of the debate about his place in contemporary English literature, at least early in his career.

Within categories like 'World Literature in English' or 'Postcolonial literature' where his hybrid provenance is not an issue, Mo is also singular, especially when compared to the increasing numbers of English-language writers of South Asian, Caribbean, or African ancestries. There is hardly another writer like him, of Anglo-Chinese provenance and a self-professed 'Brit', in the contemporary geography of literature in English. 'Creativity', Chinua Achebe once said, 'is necessarily local',[3] and a substantial amount of criticism in these fields involves the exploration of the historical and cultural specificities which writers represent, address and critique in their work. In these projects, continuities between an author's birthplace and his or her cultural affinities, allegiances and alignments are often assumed, and made the subject of critical investigation. Such continuities are actively denied by Mo himself, and in view of the global compass of his subject matter, can hardly be assumed. For Mo, where or what is the 'local'?

Primary literary categories tend to be founded on the basis of community – existing, historical or notional. We are used to speaking in terms of French, or Jewish, or Southeast Asian writing, for example. In the light of this, Mo stands apart from writers who could conceivably be bonded into a particular regional or cultural collective through comparative studies. In the fields of 'World Literature in English' or 'Postcolonial literature', the push towards a cross-national and cross-cultural critical consciousness comes up frequently against an equally strong tendency towards segregation along national or regional lines. The segregationist tendency is inextricable from a late twentieth-century movement in literary and cultural studies towards the fashioning of cultural identities which privileges ethnic heritage, often grounded on narratives of shared histories. Much postcolonial writing seem to demand to be read in this way. Mo's strenuous denial of value to 'Chineseness', and the absence of some common ethnic denominator in his fiction, go against this dominant – if problematic – paradigm.

There are four possible ways of addressing – or redressing – the current critical neglect of Mo's work. The first is an author-based study like the current work. Each of the other three approaches would involve situating Mo in a community of writers, so that together the other three approaches open up a number of aesthetic and cultural locations for him and his novels. One of these locations is diasporal Chinese fiction, in which Mo's novels may be placed in comparison and contrast with other writers of Chinese ancestry who have written in English, and especially on the experience of 'Chinese' people crossing over to cultures in the west. *Sour Sweet* is obviously the novel which best fits into a study of this kind.[4] However, Chinese diasporal fiction is not a single location, and exemplifies a plurality of histories and voices. Comparative studies of individual works or authors have to be very precisely framed in order to avoid the kind of 'misleading readings' which Rushdie has warned against, especially ones based on presumed commonalities, either in some mythical or constructed 'Chineseness' that persists despite dias-poral relocations, or in a monolithic experience of marginalisation or racism in the course of relocation. In complex ways, Mo's vantage on 'Chinese' ethnicity and culture, gleaned from all his novels, diverges significantly from, say, the Chinese-American fiction of Maxine Hong Kingston, a divergence further compli-cated by radically different positions on gender. As in *Sour Sweet*, 'Chineseness' in Maxine Hong Kingston's *The Woman Warrior* (1976) is constituted through memory, daily rituals and practices, and in family relationships, but as it emerges in the two narratives, it also takes on different forms, and challenges presumptions of ethnic integration, homogeneity or essentialism. Despite the obvious difference in the provenance of the two works, it is possible to argue that the construct of 'Chineseness' in Kingston's work is fuelled by diasporal pressures similar to those which sustain Lily Chen's resolutely 'Chinese' self-identification.[5] A comparative study would also emphasise the significance of both works as cultural performances. *The Woman Warrior* disorients received narratives of 'Americanness' to which ethnic minorities in the United States have been historically incorporated, while *Sour Sweet* alerts the British reading public to the presence among them of immigrants who resolutely refuse to be assimilated, and goes some way towards explaining – without fully endorsing – the reasons for their intransigence.

The third way would align Mo with other writers in a postcolonial community which is multi-ethnic and cannot be fixed within a single geographical location. Both Bruce King and Victor Ramraj have done pioneering work in this area, the former focusing on thematic and perspectival cross-references among the writers, while the latter, drawing upon postcolonial theories, frames his studies in terms of concepts of dislocation, hybridity and interstitial subjectivities.[6] The methodology of such studies, valuable as they are, does not allow for detailed textual discussion. Thus, a fourth approach, which has not been developed so far, would be to interface a detailed critical study of Mo's novels with broader conceptual frames that draw on the work of other writers. In this new undertaking, a comparative study of *Brownout* with other contemporary writing on the Philippines, such as James Hamilton-Paterson's *Ghosts of Manila*, James Fenton's *The Snap Revolution* (1986) and some of the poems in his *Out of Danger* (1993) and more recently Alex Garland's *The Tesseract* (1998), could illuminate the different vantages on a single geographical location that is underrepresented in contemporary British writing. At the same time, it would engage, critically and theoretically, the problematic of representation as it pertains to cross-cultural writing.

These four critical approaches testify to the multiple belongings – or locations – of Timothy Mo's creative imagination. In a book review of I. Allan Sealy's *The Trotter-Nama* (1988), Mo, with typical wit and acerbity, asserts,

> There's been a coup in the sleepy little kingdom of British fiction. The subcontinental Fabulists rose up and slaughtered the Kitchen Realists in a Night of Long Pens. Once, the majority of English novels were parochial, petty and technically unadventurous to the point of blandness. They were also overwhelmingly by Anglo-Saxon writers. They still are, but now yeasty foreign organisms pullulate in all that dough, making the loaf rise into exotic shapes.[7]

The fact that Sealy, an Anglo-Indian, is 'settled in New Zealand after an education in Michigan and British Columbia' did not prevent Mo's inclusion of him and his work in 'British fiction' and more specifically in the community of 'English novels'. If this is a rhetorical sleight of hand, it is a very polemical one, for it suggests a seamless continuity between the different locations of Sealy's experience. Strategically, not only for Sealy but for Mo himself, the review asserts both 'Britishness' and multiple belongings. Mo is, of course, one of those 'yeasty foreign organisms' he talks about, as his imagination of otherness takes shape in different locations in East and Southeast Asia. But his optic moves back, from time to time, to contemporary Britain and British fiction as the domain which, from the very beginning of his career, has felt most keenly the controversies of his work and his singular presence. In Mr Smith and Castro's adventures among the immigrant community in Plaistow, East London, *Renegade or Halo²* has Mo's most important – because the most fully detailed – contemporary British character and references to working-class Britain since *Sour Sweet*. After a number of novels set away from a British milieu, it would not be surprising if Mo next makes one of his returns, except that in his globalised fictional geography, this would figure as a return to a neglected outpost rather than an imperial or literary centre. He is one of those contemporary writers engaged in the project of turning English inside out.

Notes

Chapter 1

1 Unless otherwise indicated, all quotations from Mo's novels will be from the first edition.

2 At the moment, these writers and their fiction can be assigned to a number of overlapping academic categories – 'Commonwealth Literature', 'New Literatures in English', 'Postcolonial Literatures'. In this turn-of-the-century moment, these categories are the plural signs not only of the writers' creative vigour but also the diverse energies in their critical reception. Timothy Mo's fiction has received academic attention in all three categories. While I will be referring to critical comments on Mo and his work throughout the book, an overview of the reception of the novels will be given in the final chapter.

3 Bruce King (ed.), *New National and Post-Colonial Literatures: An Introduction*, Oxford, Clarendon Press, 1996, p. 3. King's essay, 'New Centres of Consciousness: New, Post-Colonial, and International English Literature' (3–26), provides a useful summary of the history and development of the overlapping categories of literature that he refers to in the quotation.

4 Stuart Hall, 'Cultural identity and diaspora' in Jonathan Rutherford (ed.), *Identity: Community, Culture, Difference*, London, Lawrence & Wishart, 1990, pp. 222–37. See also Stuart Hall, David Held, Tony McGrew (eds), *Modernity and its Futures*, London, Polity Press and the Open University Press, 1992, and more recently, Stuart Hall and Paul du Gay (ed.), *Questions of Cultural Identity*, London, Sage, 1996.

5 Claude Rawson, (ed.), *English Satire and the Satiric Tradition*, Oxford, Basil Blackwell, 1984, p. v.

6   Timothy Mo, 'Fighting their Writing: The unholy lingo of RLS
    and Kung Fu Tse', *New Writing 5*, Christopher Hope and Peter
    Porter (eds), London: Vintage, 1996, 299–318. An earlier, and
    shorter, version of this article which relates the formative influ-
    ence of Mr Tingle was published in Hong Kong in *Eastern Express
    Weekend*, 5 February 1994. The article is entitled 'One of Billy's
    Boys: A Memoir by Timothy Mo'. The two versions represent a
    unique venture in Mo's *œuvre*, and show off his considerable skills
    as essayist. Mo has written features for various publications, but
    none of equal length and scope as these two articles.

7   Mo has been extremely consistent in his disparagement of Chinese
    culture. This essay, published in 1996, contains views which are
    substantially unchanged from those expressed in an interview
    with Kazuo Ishiguro in 1982 in which Mo says: 'You can find out
    all about Chinese culture by looking at the martial arts and the
    way they go about organising it. Respect for the teacher, the way
    secret things are handed down, the way the schools are run like
    families, each with their own tradition… A very static culture that
    on the whole can't respond to stimulus and challenge from outside.
    [Chinese people are] just incapable of sustaining those Western
    values – freedom of the individual and all the rest of it – which I
    admire' (48–9). Kazuo Ishiguro, 'In conversation with Timothy
    Mo', *The Fiction Magazine*. vol. I, no. 4, Winter, 1982, pp. 48–50.

8   In the interview with Ishiguro, Mo said, 'there's no tradition of
    moral courage in Chinese culture', and that 'the fact that the
    family is the unit of survival, not the individual' creates a society
    'just incapable of sustaining those Western values – freedom of the
    individual … which I admire' (49), Kazuo Ishiguro, 'In Conver-
    sation with Timothy Mo'. The first part of this observation is
    repeated in an interview with Gay Firth, *The Fiction Magazine*,
    June 1986, p. 38. In 'Fighting their Writing', we can see the most
    recent restatement of this position.

9   Shu Ming, 'An Interview with Timothy Mo', *Unitas: A Literary
    Monthly* (Taiwan), vol. 7, no. 12, 1991, pp. 21–5. The interview
    was conducted in English but translated and published in Chinese.
    In the interview, Mo's Chinese name is disclosed.

10 *The Complete Works of George Orwell*, vol. 12, Peter Davison
    (ed.), London, Secker and Warburg, 1998, p. 106.

11 Rawson, *English Satire and the Satiric Tradition*, p. v. Rawson is,
    of course, thinking specifically about Augustan satire while the
    convention, in broader terms, allows for variations in which the
    'punitive and hurtful' represent the more extreme end of the range.

12   *TLS* (7 May 1982), 502.

13   *Sunday Times* (25 April 1982).

14   Ian Parker, interview with Timothy Mo, *Blitz*, July 1987, p. 34.

15   Ishiguro, 'In conversation with Timothy Mo', p. 49.

16   Cited in Christopher Tookey, 'In the china-shop', *Books and Bookmen*, May 1986, p. 8.

17   Cited in Lucy Hughes-Hallett, 'A singular obsession: Timothy Mo', *Vogue*, August 1986, p. 150.

18   Rawson, *English Satire and the Satiric Tradition*, p. v.

19   These arguments usually demonstrate, consciously or uncon-sciously, one or a number of the following: the belief in an authentic ethnic identity; a desire to return to some kind of ethnic purity after colonialism; cultural nationalism. A well-known work in the field of world literature and post-colonial literature which puts forward these arguments is Chinweizu, Jemie, Madubuike, *Toward the Decolonisation of African Literature*, London, KPI, 1985.

20   The ethnographical approach is represented by the work of James Clifford in *The Predicament of Culture*, Cambridge, Massachu-setts, Harvard University Press, 1988, and the collection of essays, *Routes: Travel and Translation in the Late Twentieth Century*, Cambridge, Massachusetts, Harvard University Press, 1997, and Arthur Krupat, *Ethnocriticism*, Berkeley and Los Angeles, Univer-sity of California Press, 1992. See also Edward Said, 'Representing the colonized: anthropology's interlocutors', *Critical Inquiry*, vol. 15, Winter, 1989, pp. 205–25.

Inspired by Frantz Fanon's *Black Skin, White Masks* (1952), translated by Charles Lam Markmann, New York, Grove, 1967, the psychoanalytical approach to studies of colonial subjectivities can be seen, for example, in Homi Bhabha, 'Remembering Fanon: self, psyche, and the colonial condition'; 'Forward' to *Black Skin, White Masks*, London, Pluto, 1986; 'Of mimicry and man: the ambivalence of colonial discourse', *October*, vol. 28, Spring 1984, pp. 125–33; 'The other question – the stereotype and colonial dis-course', *Screen*, vol. 24, no. 6, 1983, pp. 18–36; and Gail Ching-Liang Low, *White Skins/Black Masks: Representations and Colonial-ism*, London, Routledge, 1996.

In temporal–spatial approaches to cultural identities, see David Harvey's seminal work, *The Condition of Postmodernity*, Oxford, Blackwell, 1989, and more recently, *Justice, Nature and the Geography of Difference*, Oxford, Blackwell, 1996. See also Stuart

Hall, 'The question of cultural identity' in *Modernity and its Futures*, pp. 273–326. References to some of these works will be made in the studies of Mo's novels in the following chapters.

21   Detailed references to recent New Historicist theories on the writing of history, and their differences from conventional historiography will be made in the course of Chapter 4 on *An Insular Possession*.

22   Timothy Mo, 'One of Billy's Boys', p. 14.

23   For a study and critique of the dissemination of these ideas in popular British fiction for boys, see Kelly Boyd, 'Knowing your place: the tensions of manliness in boys' story papers, 1918–39' in Michael Roper and John Tosh (eds), *Manful Assertions: Masculinities in Britain since 1800*, London and New York, Routledge, 1991, pp. 145–65.

24   Timothy Mo, 'Views from the deep', *The Independent*, 27 May 1988.

25   Edward Said, *Orientalism*, New York, Pantheon, 1978; *Culture and Imperialism*, London, Chatto & Windus, 1993. See, among others, the collection of essays setting out theoretical frames and paradigms in Francis Barker, Peter Hulme and Margaret Iversen (eds), *Colonial Discourse, Post-colonial Theory*, Manchester, Manchester University Press, 1994 and Jonathan White (ed.), *Recasting the World: Writing after Colonialism*, Baltimore, Maryland, Johns Hopkins University Press, 1993 which contain essays on both American and postcolonial literatures, and David Spurr, *The Rhetoric of Empire: Colonial Discourse in Journalism, Travel Writing, and Imperial Administration*, Durham, Duke University Press, 1993, for more detailed investigations of discourse strategies.

26   Interview by Ian Parker, *Blitz*, July 1987, p. 36, italics in original.

27   See Achebe's letters in response to the criticism of the Nigerian critic, Obiajunwa Wali, in *Transition*, vol. 3, no. 11, 1963, pp. 7–9, and vol. 3, no. 12, 1964, pp. 6–10, and his essay, 'The African writer and the English language' (1964), rpt. in *Morning Yet on Creation Day*, London, Heinemann, 1975, pp. 91–103. The 'Introduction' contains a more critical stance towards the 1964 article.

28   Salman Rushdie, 'Imaginary Homelands' (1982), rpt. in *Imaginary Homelands: Essays and Criticism 1981–1991*, London, Granta and Penguin, 1991, p. 17.

29   While Rushdie's writing has often been compared to the magic realism of South American novelists, and Rushdie himself has

written enthusiastic reviews about the novels of Gabriel Garcia Márquez and Maria Vargas Llosa (*Imaginary Homelands*, 299–317), Mo professes his dislike of the Latin-American novel 'as a form of representing reality', and complains of what he calls the 'degraded, fantastical vision' in Márquez's novels. See Ian Parker, p. 34.

30   Shu Ming, 'An Interview with Timothy Mo', p. 25.

31   Timothy Mo, 'Fighting their Writing', p. 299.

32   V. S. Naipaul, 'New clothes: an unwritten story' in *A Way in the World*, London, Minerva, 1994, pp. 45–6.

Chapter 2

1   Quotations from *The Monkey King* refer to the paperback edition, London, Abacus, 1984.

2   Mo used 'Macau' in *The Monkey King* and 'Macao' in *An Insular Possession* and *The Redundancy of Courage*, perhaps to take into account the fact that the latter two novels have an earlier historical time-frame than the first.

3   Here, I would like to follow Robert Young, and distinguish the nineteenth-century use of the word 'hybridity' to describe a physiological phenomenon from its contemporary use in cultural theories. Young, *Colonial Desire: Hybridity in Theory, Culture and Race*, London and New York, Routledge, 1995. Mo is describing a 'Macau' in the 1950s and early 1960s in which cultural hybridity has yet to follow the racial mixture of Portuguese and Chinese. In his representation, 'Macau' appears as a fictional 'contact zone', a theoretical term, derived from studies of creolised languages, coined by Mary Louis Pratt in her system-oriented study of colonial cultures. Pratt, *Imperial Eyes: Travel Writing and Transculturation*, London and New York, Routledge, 1992. The dialectic of thesis–antithesis–synthesis which informs Pratt's study can be seen in Mo's 'Macau' where the meeting and mingling of Chinese and Portuguese peoples and languages have produced a third subject, a Macanese like Wallace, who nonetheless continues to think and act out the historical legacy of colonial conflict. In some sense, the novel can be seen as working towards the kind of cultural synthesis which Pratt identifies in her study but it also shows how the first two terms of the dialectic – thesis–antithesis, or Chinese-Portuguese – are also transformed in the process.

4   Austin Coates's *City of Broken Promises*, 1967, rpt. Oxford, Oxford University Press, 1987, set in Macau, is one of the few fictional works available which offer insights into the ethnic tensions of the Portuguese colony. For more recent work which explores 'Macau' as the site and space in which Chinese, Portuguese and other cultures negotiate in uneven symmetry, see Jonathan Porter, *Macau: The Imaginary City*, Boulder, Colorado, Westview Press, 1996, and Christina Cheng Miu-bing, 'Macau: A Cultural Janus in Colonial Vicissitudes', unpublished doctoral thesis, University of Hong Kong, 1996. 'Macau' is the currently accepted spelling for the name of the enclave, while 'Macao' is the Portuguese-inflected traditional name.

5   Northrop Frye, *Anatomy of Criticism: Four Essays*, Princeton, New Jersey, Princeton University Press, 1957, rpt. 1971, pp. 43, 164. Frye's observations about archetypes, with their universalist assumptions, may seem inappropriate as an entry to our understanding of Mo's novel which is set in a radically different Chinese cultural milieu. But one must not forget that in its formal properties, Mo's novel can and should be situated in a western tradition of comic realism which it was part of Frye's project to theorise. At various moments in this book, I will be referring to classic studies of generic forms like Frye's work or, as earlier on in Chapter 1, the work of Claude Rawson on satire. Such references situate Mo's novels vis-à-vis particular conventions, and in doing so, offer structural vantages from which our critical discussions can begin.

6   The authorship of *Hsi-yu Chi*, published in 1592, is usually ascribed to the Ming dynasty writer Wu Cheng-en. For a complete English translation of the work, with scholarly notes and full textual apparatus, see Anthony C. Yu (transl. and ed.), *The Journey to the West*, 4 vols, Chicago, University of Chicago Press, 1977–1983. To date, the most popular and textually accessible translation remains Arthur Waley's abridged *Monkey*, London, Allen & Unwin, 1942.

7   It is interesting to note that Chinese scholars have sourced the prototype of Monkey, or Sun Wu-kung, in foreign literatures, especially Hanumat and his adventures in *Ramayana*. See Yu, *The Journey to the West*, p. 498, n. 30. Monkey not only hybridises different and conflictual discourses within Chinese culture, but in his conception, also crosses the boundaries between Chinese and other cultures.

8   Frye, *Anatomy of Criticism*, p.44.

9   Raymond Williams, *The Long Revolution*, New York, Columbia University Press, 1961, p. 277.

10   John Rothfork's essay, 'Confucianism in Timothy Mo's *The Monkey King*', *World Literature Written in English*, vol. 29, no. 2, 1989, pp. 50–61 examines the novel as a 'fictional critique of Confucian ethics' (50). It is an interesting approach but it does tend to perpetuate dichotomies between the 'Confucian' and the 'Western' which reduce both to a preconceived, and largely stable, corpus of characteristics. In this respect, Rothfork is, ironically, not unlike Mo.

11   Frye, *Anatomy of Criticism*, pp. 166–7.

Chapter 3

1   Quotations from *Sour Sweet* refer to the paperback edition, London, Abacus, 1989.

2   Hall, 'Cultural Identity and Diaspora', p. 222. For a study of the tradition and aesthetics of the realist novel, see Wayne Booth, *The Rhetoric of Fiction*, and more recently, Dennis Walder (ed.), *The Realist Novel*, London, Routledge and the Open University Press, 1995.

3   Timothy Mo, 'From the Mines of Curry Powder: A review of I. Allan Sealy's *The Trotter-Nama*', *New York Times*, 28 February 1988. In the review, Mo acknowledges the achievements of the 'Subcontinental Fabulists' of whom Sealy is one. But he judges Sealy's novel as wanting on a number of counts which suggest his own realist preoccupations: a narrative full of interpolations which strives for 'sophistication of construction' but only ends up in being shapeless; characters so lacking in detail that they cannot engage a reader's interest; and unsuccessful attempts at wit. Mo concludes that Sealy's effort actually makes him miss the realism which the fabulist mode sets out to deconstruct.

4   Khachig Tölölian, 'The nation state and its others: in lieu of a preface', *Diaspora*, vol. I, no. 1, 1991, pp. 4–5.

5   Victor Ramraj has suggested that Man Kee 'will begin with a new clean slate', and quotes from a moment in *Sour Sweet*, at the end of Chapter Fourteen, in support of his statement. 'Diasporas and Multiculturalism' in King (ed.), *New National and Post-Colonial Literatures*, p. 225. While it is true that the narrator observes that Man Kee would have 'no history, no heritage to live up to, no goal to fulfil, no ancient burden to carry' (111), Ramraj neglected to include his final comment, which is also the last sentence of the

chapter: 'Not one his father imposed, anyway.' The implication of this comment, in terms of Man Kee's potentially difficult matri-archal inheritance, is clear.

6   I am here adapting, and transposing to the study of individual sub-jectivity, Raymond Williams's observation about 'the formation of a new class, the coming to consciousness of a new class, and within this, in actual process, the (often uneven) emergence of elements of a new cultural formation'. R. Williams, *Marxism and Literature*, Oxford, Oxford University Press, 1977, p. 124.

7   A rare example is *Exploring Our Chinese Identity*, Michelle Lacey, Lili Man and Jessie Lim (eds), London, Lambeth Chinese Community Association, 1992. This is a collection of creative writing by young writers of Chinese ancestry who have lived most of their lives in Britain, and shows that their understanding of what it means to be 'Chinese' on the one hand, and their experience of 'Britain' on the other, are by no means homogenous, and are very much inflected by family and regional differences.

8   See Suk-Tak Tam, 'Representations of "the Chinese" and "Ethnicity" in British Racial Discourse', in Elizabeth Sinn (ed.), *The Last Half Century of Chinese Overseas*, Hong Kong, Hong Kong University Press, 1988, pp. 81–90. Tam is particularly critical of James Watson's influential article, 'The Chinese, Hong Kong Villagers in the British Catering Trade', in Watson (ed.), *Between Two Cultures: Migrants and Minorities in Britain*, Oxford, Blackwell, 1977, pp. 181–213. Note that Watson's article only predates *Sour Sweet* by five years, and the two publications, though in different genres, can be said to belong to the same period. A more considered study of the recent history of the Chinese in Britain as it is mediated by oral narratives is David Parker's 'Emerging British Chinese Identities: Issues and Problems' in Sinn (ed.), *The Last Half Century of Chinese Overseas*, pp. 91–114, which is a summarised extract from his earlier book, *Through Different Eyes: The Cultural Identities of Young Chinese People in Britain*, Aldershot, Avebury, 1995.

9   Of course, satirising a taste for violence for its own sake, by describing it, is a potentially compromised activity. A similar ambivalence can be detected in the way Mo speaks about boxing as a spectator sport. 'I am a shrinking violet,' he once said, 'who goes nowhere and sees no one for five days a week, then I go to a boxing match – and people shout and swear at me. I love it.' Hunter Davies, 'Making the Chinese Scrutable', *Sunday Times*, 23 January 1983. A few years later, in another interview, he calls boxing 'a grisly sport', and adds, 'I've had people ringing me up in the middle of the night to say, "I'm going to break your arms and

legs." It's a very horrible business.' But in the same breath, he says, 'I love to go to a boxing match and be jostled and sock someone back. It's such a change from sitting in that chair writing novels.' Lucy Hughes-Hallett, 'A Singular Obsession: Timothy Mo', p. 151. The dismemberment he was threatened with is fictionalised in the triad wars in *Sour Sweet*. Mo's personal relish for a violent encounter at a boxing match is as obvious as his repulsion by the violence innate in boxing as a sport and in the culture which has grown around it. He likes and loathes boxing, because it is violent, in the same way that the pleasure in writing about violence and the critique of violence as an end in itself go together in *Sour Sweet*.

10   Ishiguro, 'In Conversation with Timothy Mo', p. 49.

11   See, for example, Gayatri Chakravorty Spivak, 'Can the Subaltern Speak?' in C. Nelson and L. Grossberg (eds), *Marxism and the Interpretation of Culture*, Basingstoke, Macmillan, 1988, pp. 271–313, and the collection of essays which critique monologic and monolithic discourses of the nation-state in Homi Bhabha (ed.), *Nation and Narration*, London, Routledge, 1990.

12   Ian McEwan, *Soursweet*, London, Faber, 1988, p. x.

13   *Soursweet*, directed by Mike Newell, London, First Film Company, 1988.

14   McEwan, *Soursweet*, p. ix.

15   See David Parker's 'Emerging British Chinese identities: issues and problems', and *Through Different Eyes: The Cultural Identities of Young Chinese People in Britain*, for detailed discussion of new British Chinese subjectivities. Parker makes skilful use of references to artistic and cultural productions.

16   McEwan, *Soursweet*, p. x.

Chapter 4

1   An earlier version of this chapter has appeared as an article entitled 'How not to write history: Timothy Mo's *An Insular Possession*', *ARIEL: A Review of International English Literature*, vol. 24, no. 3, 1994, pp. 51–65. I would like to thank the editors of *ARIEL* for giving me permission to include material from the article.

2   Edward Said talks about the great rivers in nineteenth-century narratives that codify and reproduce what he calls 'a structure of attitude and reference' which, in turn, forms the cultural bedrock

of the imperial enterprise and its enduring legacy. Edward Said, *Culture and Imperialism*, London, Chatto & Windus, 1993, p. 73 *passim*. See especially Chapter 1, parts 1 and 2.

3   Parker, *Blitz*. July 1987, p. 34.

4   Parker, *Blitz*. July 1987, p. 34. Italics in original.

5   While Mo's admission of the mixture of fact and fiction in his novel is clear, it is much more difficult to say precisely what he means by 'sincerity'. In his statements, 'sincerity' is cognate to 'truthful', but also implicitly opposed to 'truthfulness' as absolute adherence to facts. Traditionally, the word 'sincere' has to mediate two sets of relations: the first set concerns the author and the external, objectively ascertainable world, and the second, the author and his creative intents and desires. The pressures from these two sets of relations are quite often conflicting, thus generating a field of ambivalence which accrues round the word 'sincerity'. Literature and the self-identity of authors thrive on this ambivalence, and its richness, historical density and multiplying complications are the subject of Lionel Trilling's classic study, *Sincerity and Authenticity*, New York, Norton, 1969. Trilling also discusses the displacement of 'sincerity' by 'authenticity' in which the loyalty to an individualised identity, rather than to inner moral feelings shared with others, is paramount. In other words, it is the second set of relations mentioned above which became historically ascendant in framing the writer's sense of self-worth and self-identity, and the value of his art. In the absence of clarification from Mo, and in view of what he has done in *An Insular Possession*, it can be argued that he has privileged 'sincerity' in the second set of relations, that is, to imply truthfulness of his work to the self and its way of being. And by showing that historical 'fact' can be produced, constructed and manufactured, he implicitly dismisses the question of 'sincerity' from the first set of relations between the author and an objectively ascertainable world.

   More recently, in the context of debates about multiculturalism, Charles Taylor has drawn on the humanist heritage in Trilling's work in order to talk about the 'ideal of authenticity' which guarantees the politics of recognition and the mutual respect of the culturally different. See Taylor, 'The politics of recognition', in Amy Gutman (ed.), *Multiculturalism*, Princeton, New Jersey, Princeton University Press, 1994, pp. 25–74.

6   For a study of naming, and its importance in colonial discourse, see Mary Louise Pratt, *Imperial Eyes: Travel Writing and Transculturation,*. London and New York, Routledge, 1992.

7   The American merchants were not at all disinterested in the British preoccupations with trade and commerce. (See Jonathan D. Spence, *The Chan's Great Continent: China in Western Minds*, New York, W. W. Norton, 1998.) But in making Chase and Eastman journalists rather than traders, Mo clearly wishes to bracket them off from the aggressive pursuit of commercial profits, British and American. Edward Said also reminds us of the 'imperial cast' of much of American writing in the first half of the nineteenth century – 'the Puritan "errand into the wilderness" ... expansion westward, along with the wholesale colonization and destruction of native American life' – which is paradoxical to its 'ferocious anti-colonialism, directed at the Old World'. *Culture and Imperialism*, pp. 74–5.

8   See especially *Tropics of Discourse*, Baltimore, Maryland, Johns Hopkins University Press, 1978, and 'Historical Pluralism', *Critical Inquiry*, vol. 12, no. 3 , 1986, pp. 480–93.

9   Louis A. Montrose, 'Professing the Renaissance: The Poetics and Politics of Culture', in H. Aram Veeser (ed.), *The New Historicism*, New York and London, Routledge, 1989.

10   In a recent article, John McLeod takes issue with this particular moment of my argument in the earlier version of this chapter published as 'How not to write history: Timothy Mo's *An Insular Possession*'. McLeod, 'On the chase for Gideon Nye: history and representation in Timothy Mo's *An Insular Possession*', *Journal of Commonwealth Literature*, pp. 61–73. McLeod is resourceful in his use of archival material, and I am persuaded by his identification of Gideon Nye as the historical referent of Gideon Chase. But his disagreement with my article is a function of distortion. In focusing on one particular moment, he completely ignores my central argument on the political project of *An Insular Possession* which is the critique of the dominant discourses of imperialism that frame and determine historiography and the agency of Chase as translator. McLeod warns against postmodernist readings which depoliticise the novel – a project which he insists on ascribing to my article. But if he has taken my entire article on board, he cannot fail to see that his contention that Chase contests the '*historical a priori* of Western knowledge in Hong Kong' (68), but cannot in the end liberate himself from its power, maps onto my earlier argument. The following two quotations, one from my article, another from McLeod's give an example of this mapping. In my article, I argued, 'Chase's implicit attempts at shaping history come up inevitably against the power of dominant discourses... In Chase's implicit lament at his loss of credibility,

the novel, as a critique of how history is made, retreats from any privileging of an attempt at hybridised discourse. The Chinese and British reactions enact the closure by violence of a historical process, the dynamics of which, from the point of view of the radical outsider, are textual negotiation. The novel in the end distinguishes between the forms of power that control the making of history' (59). McLeod: 'In *An Insular Possession*, then, the dominant system of enunciability or *historical a priori* is foregrounded by calling attention to the ways it gives meaning to the statements that are made within it. Chase's knowledge is chiefly valuable for the purposes of conflict, rather than other kinds of cross-cultural conflict. Neither Gideon's anti-postmodern attempt to find "perfect correspondence" between Western and Chinese cultures, nor the postmodern revelation that representation is "accepted fiction", can successfully challenge the power of the *historical a priori*' (71).

11   In a 1993 article, 'The empire writes back', *Time*, 8 February 1993, pp.48–53, Pico Iyer discusses Mo and other novelists such as Salman Rushdie, Kazuo Ishiguro, Ben Okri and Michael Ondaatje in terms of their cross-cultural mobility which throws up the subject matter and generates the creative energy of their fiction. *The Empire Writes Back* is, of course, the title of an earlier, and quite different, critical–theoretical work, where cultural retrieval and reconstruction and the imagination of origins are given prominence as major paradigms of postcolonial fiction. Apart from a few writers such as Rushdie, who feature in both publications, each tends to draw together a different group of writers and corpus of writing. Bill Ashcroft et al. (eds), *The Empire Writes Back*, New York and London, Routledge, 1989.

Chapter 5

1   Quotations from *The Redundancy of Courage* refer to the paperback edition, London, Vintage, 1992. This chapter has gone through two earlier versions, the first as a conference paper presented at the University of Waikato, New Zealand, and then as an article, 'Satire and the National Body: Timothy Mo's *The Redundancy of Courage*', published in *SPAN*: Journal of the South Pacific Association of Commonwealth Literature and Language Studies. I would like to thank the editors of *SPAN* for permission to include material from the article.

2   For information on the history and recent political struggle in East Timor, see, among others, Jose Ramos-Hortu, *Funu – the Unfinished Saga of East Timor*, New Jersey, Red Sea Press, 1987; John Taylor, *Indonesia's Forgotten War: The Hidden History of East Timor*, London, Zed Books, 1991; and Sonny Inbaraj, *East Timor: Blood and Tears in ASEAN* (1995), Thailand, Silkwork Books, 1997.

3   It is not known if Mo has consulted any of the books on East Timor in n. 2 above. However, as an instructor for the Scuba Diving Association in Britain, he has led expeditions for diving enthusiasts in Southeast Asia, and has visited a number of countries in the region including Indonesia, Singapore, Malaysia, the Philippines and Thailand.

4   Benedict Anderson, *Imagined Communities*, London, Verso, 1983, rpt. 1989, p. 15.

5   ' "Of all the novels I've written, this is the one I like least," Mo says. "It wasn't much fun to write and it's not a book I'd much like to read."' Interview with Jill McGivering, *South China Morning Post*, 20 April 1991. See also Kate Kellaway, 'Bang and whoosh, crack and thump', *The Observer*, 14 April 1991. Of Ng, Mo, in a revealing statement which partially explains his dislike, says, 'I don't like him... He's like a rat, continually resurfacing after the dust has settled. He's my nightmare of what I might be.' Kate Pullinger, 'Creating a hero of our times', *Sunday Times*, 14 April 1991.

6   These three temporal moments are translated into fictional themes and theorised by the authors (Bill Ashcroft et al.) of *The Empire Writes Back*, London, Routledge, 1989. Elleke Boehmer's *Colonial and Post-colonial Literature*, Oxford, Oxford University Press, 1995, studies continuities between fictional literature from different global locations which explore common themes and time-frames shaped by the historical processes of colonialism and decolonisation. It is less theoretical than *The Empire Writes Back* but offers better critical insights.

7   Anderson, *Imagined Communities*, p.13.

8   Bhabha, *Nation and Narration*, 'Introduction: narrating the nation', pp. 1–7.

9   There is an uncanny and disturbing resemblance between Ng's voice and the testimony of a Chinese trader from Dili, East Timor, to Amnesty International on the Indonesian invasion in 1975: 'People started screaming, saying they were civilians, not political. One person, Tsam I Tin, who had come to Dili from Same, came out of the house next to the Toko Lay to surrender and was shot dead. His son came out also and was also shot but not fatally. He

pretended to be dead and survived. The Indonesians then broke into the building and told everyone to come out... All of us were taken, including my wife who was pregnant, and my child. When we were in front of the Sporting Club, we were made to sit in line. The Indonesians made as though they were going to shoot at us but did not fire. When people cried out, the Indonesians ordered us to walk on for about 50 metres down towards the harbour. We were told to stop again and to face the sea. The taller ones were told to stand in front, the shorter ones behind. Again they cocked their rifles and made as if to fire. Then they made us walk toward the harbour gate. Again they cocked their rifles and the people were scared again.' cited in Vaudine England, 'Chinese legacy of fear in Dili', *South China Morning Post* (Hong Kong), 30 August 1999. See also 'Testimonies from two East Timorese refugees', Amnesty International ASA 21/150/99, 14 September 1999.

10   Gilbert Highet, in a standard work on satire, its form, history and taxonomy, classifies Joyce's *Ulysses* under 'Types of Literary Parody: Epic'. Highet, *The Anatomy of Satire*, Princeton, Princeton University Press, 1962.

11   The nineteenth-century western European experience of nation-building presents models of the nation that supersede ethnic differences and divisions, and these models have been adopted by some of the former colonies like India, Nigeria and Singapore as they became independent. However, such differences and the tension they generate continue to vex the nations after independence, and increasingly break out into conflict (see Clifford Geertz, 'The Integrative Revolution: Primordial Sentiments and Civil Politics in the New States', in *Old Societies and New States*, New York, Free Press, 1963, pp. 107–13) leading to calls for a return to pre-nineteenth-century poly-ethnic norms (see William H. McNeill, *Ethnicity and National Unity in World History*, Toronto, University of Toronto Press, 1986), reattuning to what a unitary nation has silenced and marginalised (see Partha Chatterjee, *The Nation and its Fragments*, Princeton, Princeton University Press, 1993), or a radical reconceptualising of the 'nation' as the in-between space of homogenising and differentiating discourses (see Bhabha (ed.), *Nation and Narration*, 'Introduction').

12   Ernest Renan, 'What is a Nation?' in Bhabha (ed.), *Nation and Narration*, p. 20.

13   Claude Rawson's *Satire and Sentiment 1660–1830*, Cambridge, Cambridge University Press, 1993, offers an informative account of the classical and English Augustan criticism of satire's impropriety directed at, among other things, its figurations of the body.

14   According to John Hutchinson, cultural nationalists see the nation as an organic entity and its essence in 'a distinctive civilization, which is the product of its unique history, cultural and geographical profile' while to 'political nationalists', the ideal nation 'is a civic *polity* of educated citizens united by common laws and mores'. J. D. Hutchinson and Anthony D. Smith (eds), *Nationalism*, Oxford, Oxford University Press, 1994, p. 12, emphasis in original. The *mestizos* exhibit both these characteristics in their bonding which significantly excludes Ng.

15   Continuing his disparagement of Chinese culture, Mo also relocates his target regionally: 'If you're talking about cultural characteristics,' he says in an interview, 'then I do think the Chinese in Southeast Asia are rapacious, selfish, non-political and no, I don't think courage is a characteristic they have either.' *South China Morning Post*, 20 April 1991. This specific reference to Southeast Asian Chinese is absent in the interviews given to London newspapers which I have consulted; the fact that it is printed in a Hong Kong newspaper with wide regional circulation would better guarantee that it would reach precisely those whom Mo targets. The *South China Morning Post* had, of course, decided to maximize this dubious appeal by headlining the interview, 'Mo's novel approach to Chinese character'. As a provocation, the comment and the novel have met with tempestuous response in a second review of the book – one more than is normal – in the *South China Morning Post*, 9 June 1991. (The first review, 'Anti-hero running with hopeless cause', was on 20 April.) Though Mo's views are entirely consistent, there is an unspoken, and perhaps unwitting, complicity between author, interviewer and reviewer, to generate maximum publicity for the novel in his birthplace where Mo claims he does 'not have a readership'. *South China Morning Post*, 20 April 1991. Again characteristically, Mo professes to be uninterested in what the press and public think about him and his latest novel, while giving the newspaper the kind of provocative statements which would make it and its readers interested in him and his work. It is tempting to say that the cynicism which Adolph Ng expresses about the media in *Redundancy* represents a function of the author's own entanglement with the press right from the start of his career.

16   *Nation and Narration*, p. 2.

17   Andrew Parker et al. (eds), *Nationalisms and Sexualities*, New York and London, Routledge, 1992, p. 5.

18   Ron Blaber, 'Dialogic on Imperialism: *The Redundancy of Courage*', *CRNLE Reviews Journal*, no. 1, 1992, pp. 31–3.

19   Tariq Ali, review of *The Redundancy of Courage*, *The Guardian*,
     18 April 1991.

20   Shirley Lim sees in Ng and Lily 'the inextinguishable identity of
     the individual', and the need to preserve and liberate the individual
     subject 'as the only defense against the violence of the collectivity,
     whether it is the collectivity of the Confucianist family, the Triad
     society, or the totalitarian state'. Lim, 'Who do we name when we
     say "diaspora"?: race, national identity, and the subject of the
     subject in Timothy Mo's novels', *Writing S.E. Asia in English:
     Against the Grain*, London, Skoob Books, 1994, p.101. While
     Lim's focus magnifies the agency of the liberated, diasporic subject
     in the novel, Rajiva Wijesinha, looking in another direction at the
     question of national identity, argues differently. Wijesinha argues
     that though Ng's 'individual identity transcends the various adjust-
     ments it has to make' (29), it is counterpointed by the identity of
     the nation of Danu which is shown to be historically contingent
     and vulnerable. Wijesinha, 'Timothy Mo's *The Redundancy of
     Courage*: An Outsider's View of Identity', *The Journal of Common-
     wealth Literature*, vol. 28, no. 1, 1993, pp. 28–33.

21   Jill McGivering, *South China Morning Post*, 20 April 1991.

22   The year when *Redundancy* was published – 1991 – seemed to have
     witnessed the final chapter of East Timor as a nation when the resist-
     ance leader, Xanana Gusmao, was sentenced to life imprisonment
     by his Indonesian captors. As I approach the closing of my chapter,
     and the ending of Mo's novel, news comes of Gusmao's transfer
     from jail to special detention in Jakarta. An unfinished story.

23   For instance, Nicholas Lezard in a review of the paperback issue of
     Redundancy in *Irish Times*, 25 June 1997, states that Mo's novel
     'helped to begin the process of opening the west's eyes' to the East
     Timor question. Similarly, in a *Guardian* review, 30 January 1997,
     it is said that *Redundancy* 'might have helped jog people's memories
     of East Timor'. Earlier, writing on Sonny Inbaraj's *East Timor:
     Blood and Tears* (See n. 1) in the *Daily Yomiuri* (Tokyo), C. J. John-
     son quoted from *Redundancy* in an implicit alignment of Mo's
     novel with Inbaraj's work.

Chapter 6

 1   The most detailed reports can be found in *Evening Standard*, 21
     March 1995, *The Scotsman*, 22 March 1995 and *The Independent*,
     8 April 1995. The excremental Prologue may help to explain the

name Mo gave to his Press, which is, of course, also self-mocking.

2   Gay Firth. 'Timothy Mo Interviewed: *An Insular Possession*', *The Fiction Magazine*, 1986, pp. 38–9.

3   Timothy Mo. 'Views from the Deep', *The Independent*, 27 May 1988.

4   See, for example, reviews by Hugo Barnacle, 'Missing the Mo juste', *Evening Standard*, 10 April 1995, and Peter Bradshaw, 'Messy tale of a modern Imelda', *The Independent*, 15 April 1995, and Susannah Herbert's plaintive 'Why books are so full of mistakes', *Sunday Telegraph*, 28 May 1995. Commenting on these mishaps, Mo says, 'I'm going to go pale with rage and grit my teeth when people say it's not as professionally edited and written as the other ones. I'll do my nut. But I really don't think that's true.' Nick Lezard, 'Self-publish and be damned', *The Independent*, 8 April 1995.

5   Speaking of the experience, Mo says, ' "It was a very bad feeling. It was like I was committing suicide as a writer. But it was a bit like jumping into an icy pool – you get used to it. Every day that has gone by I've felt more sanguine about it, until about six months ago I was figuratively jumping up and down with glee because I was doing it myself… I'm just so pleased that I did it. Number one, it's going to be in my material interests. Number two, I really like doing it – and what's in your material interests isn't necessarily what you like." He pauses, and then says, with insouciant wistfulness: "I feel sorry for other authors, actually." ' *The Independent*, 8 April 1995.

6   In this context, a useful starting point would be Andy Beckett's article, organised around an interview with Mo, which looks at the novelist's career in the context of structural changes in the publishing industry from the late 1970s. 'Sour-sweet relationships', *The Independent*, 16 April 1995.

7   This is even more noticeable if we compare *Brownout* with James Hamilton-Paterson's *Ghosts of Manila*, published two years earlier in 1994, which shows a society haunted by a colonial past running amok as the dead and corrupt assume power over the living, both locals and visitors alike. In *Brownout*, Mo makes a passing reference to Hamilton-Paterson's earlier novel, *Playing with Water* (141), but the reference is by no means a flattering one. Hamilton-Paterson's novel is mentioned in the same breath as *Hitler's War*, written by the historian and fascist apologist, David Irving, as the two books favoured by Professor Pfeidwengeler who sees in them 'models of the sturdily individual Anglo-Saxon brilliance [he] so much admired' (159).

8   The novel was praised in the Philippines English language press
    precisely because it was seen as not afraid to 'offend others, most
    especially some sensitive Filipinos who think novels written by
    foreigners with the Philippines as setting should read as glowingly
    as a DOT brochure'. Alfred Yuson, 'That brownout novel (I)',
    Philippine Daily Inquirer, 9 July 1995. See also Isabel Taylor
    Escoda, 'Who is Timothy Mo?', *Sunday Inquirer Magazine*, 18
    February 1996, which observes how Mo 'has a genuine feel for
    Filipino mores'. Escoda, a Filipina resident in Hong Kong, is also
    much more enthusiastic about Mo's early novels on the Chinese
    than most Hong Kong reviewers.

9   This sly backward reference can be found in *Renegade or Halo²*,
    p.28.

10 In a review of *Brownout*, *The Observer*, 9 April 1995, the novelist
    Helen Dunmore comments on the absence of 'pain' in Mo's
    depiction, especially in scenes like the Prologue and the injury of
    Jingkee's daughter where women appear as victims. This is
    germane not only to this novel, but also to *Renegade or Halo²* as
    we shall see. The apologies from convention, that Mo has written a
    different novel, one as robust and pain-free as Fielding's *Tom
    Jones*, goes some way towards answering Dunmore, especially in
    the context of the narrow range of sensibilities represented in
    Boyet and his world. In relation to *Renegade or Halo²*, Dunmore's
    comment would have hit much more significant keys, and called
    into doubt the credibility of the first-person narrator.

11 It is interesting to note that for the first time, Mo is called a 'right-
    wing' novelist. See Alain de Botton, review of *Brownout*, *Sunday
    Telegraph*, 27 April 1997. The novel is considered by D. J. Taylor
    as 'a near-perfect example of right-wing art' and Taylor concurs
    with de Botton in considering Mo as a novelist who 'comes from
    the Right'. Taylor, 'What a carve-up', *The Independent*, 19 April
    1997. Several reviewers also note that the novel would be
    considered politically incorrect. Such labelling, though handy for
    journalistic purposes, does not really do justice to the slippery
    political subtexts of Mo's novels.

12 David Harvey's seminal work, *The Condition of Postmodernity*,
    Oxford, Blackwell, 1990, investigates the links between economics
    and culture in the late twentieth-century world particularly in the
    way notions of time and space have been radically changed by
    global technology and the more invisible processes of global
    capitalism. Harvey offers both a history and a critique of post-
    modernism.

13   The 'Second World' refers to Soviet-bloc countries in the 'Three Worlds Theory' which has been in circulation, and seen many variant versions, since the 1950s. For a succinct critique of 'Three Worlds Theory' germane to the study of literature and culture, see Aijaz Ahmad, 'Literary theory and Third World literature: Some Contexts' in *In Theory: Classes, Nations, Literatures*, London, Verso, 1992, pp. 43–72. See also Chapter 8, 'Three Worlds Theory: End of a debate', pp. 287–318.

14   'An Interview with Timothy Mo.' *Unitas: A Literary Monthly*. p. 22. Translation mine.

Chapter 7

1   The question of complicity has been taken up by another Filipino writer before Mo. In his introduction to *Underground in Japan* (Rey Ventura's first-person account of his experience as an illegal worker in Tokyo), James Fenton notes how it came as surprise to him to learn from Ventura that 'it was not the homeless and unemployed of the Philippines who sought work abroad, but precisely the people who already had some marginal advantage in the economy' (x). In the fact of going abroad, these men acquire status in Philippines society. Ventura is unsparing in his account of their conduct, as he is sober about making visible their plight as victims of exploitation and racism. His book is, in many ways, a forerunner and companion to Mo's novel. Reynald B. Ventura, *Underground in Japan*, London, Jonathan Cape, 1992.

2   See Chapter 5, note 5.

3   The other two being Sophocles's *Oedipus Tyrannus*, and Ben Jonson's *The Alchemist*. *The Table Talk and Omniana of Samuel Taylor Coleridge*, T. Ashe (ed.), London, George Bell, 1901, pp. 295–6.

4   See Edward Said's discussion of 'radical typing' in *Orientalism*, Chapter 3, Part II.

5   Boyd Tonkin, 'Postcards from the edge', *The Independent*, 10 July 1999.

6   Timothy Mo, 'They will not apologise', *Daily Telegraph*, 7 March 1998.

7   Timothy Mo, 'They will not apologise', *Daily Telegraph*, 7 March 1998.

Chapter 8

1 See John Rothfork's articles referred to in Chapter Two, note 10.

2 ' "Commonwealth Literature" does not exist' (1983), rpt. in *Imaginary Homelands: Essays and Criticism 1981–1991*, London, Granta Books, 1991, p. 64.

3 Chinua Achebe, *Morning Yet on Creation Day*, p. 26.

4 See my article, 'Of laundries and restaurants: fictions of ethnic space', *Wasafiri*, vol. 21, 1995, pp. 16–19.

5 In the context of the South Asian diaspora, Amitav Ghosh has argued that the desire to return to an originary homeland is not as obvious as the re-creation of an ethnic culture in new locations. Ghosh, 'The diaspora in Indian culture', *Public Culture*, vol. I, no. 1, 1989, pp. 73–8. It can be said that Ghosh's two terms articulate a significant difference between *Sour Sweet* and *The Woman Warrior*, though in Mo's novel, the former is very much a conscious driving force which also generates the dynamic of the latter in a relationship that Lily is only partly aware of.

6 See the work of Bruce King and Victor Ramraj referred to earlier on in Chapters 1 and 2. See also Shirley Lim's, 'Who do we name when we say "diaspora"?: race, national identity, and the subject of the subject in Timothy Mo's novels'.

7 Timothy Mo, 'From the Mines of Curry Powder: *The Trotter-Nama* by I. Allan Sealy', *New York Times*, 28 February 1988.

Select bibliography

Works by Timothy Mo

FICTION

The Monkey King, London, André Deutsch, 1978.

Sour Sweet, London, André Deutsch, 1982.

An Insular Possession, London, Chatto & Windus, 1986.

The Redundancy of Courage, London, Chatto & Windus, 1991.

Brownout on Breadfruit Boulevard, London, Paddleless Press, 1995.

Renegade or Halo², London, Paddleless Press, 1999

ARTICLES AND BOOK REVIEWS

'Hsia Chih-yen's *The Coldest Winter in Peking* and Anthony Grey's *The Chinese Assassin*', *Sunday Times*, 17 September 1978.

'Views from the deep', *The Independent*, 27 May 1988.

'Second thoughts', *The Independent*, 8 May 1993.

'One of Billy's Boys', *Eastern Express Weekend* (Hong Kong), 5 February 1994.

'Fighting their Writing: The unholy lingo of RLS and Kung Fu Tse', Christopher Hope and Peter Porter (eds), *New Writing 5*, London, Vintage, 1996, pp. 299–318.

'Why can't they write better novels?', review of *Traveller's Literary Companion: Southeast Asia*, Alastair Dingwall (ed.), *The Spectator*, 6 January 1996.

'From the mines of curry powder', *The New York Times*, 28 February 1988.

'They will not apologise', *Daily Telegraph*, 7 March 1998.

Film Adaptation

McEwan, Ian, *Soursweet*, London, Faber, 1988.

Newell, Mike, director of *SourSweet*, London, First Film Company, 1988.

Interviews with Timothy Mo

Beckett, Andy, 'Sour-sweet relationships', *The Independent*, 16 April 1995.

Billson, Anne, 'Timothy Mo: the non-history man', *Time Out*, 8–15 April 1986.

Blaine, Garth, 'The real thing', *Harpers*, May 1982.

Davies, Hunter, 'Making the Chinese scrutable', *Sunday Times*, 23 January 1983.

Firth, Gay, 'Timothy Mo interviewed: *An Insular Possession*', *The Fiction Magazine*, July 1986, pp. 37–9.

Herbert, Hugh, 'Families which prey together…' *The Guardian*, 21 June 1983.

Hughes-Hallett, Lucy, 'A singular obsession: Timothy Mo', *Vogue*, August 1986.

Ishiguro, Kazuo, 'In conversation with Timothy Mo', *The Fiction Magazine*, Winter, 1982, pp. 48–50.

Kellaway, Kate, 'Bang and Whoosh, Crack and Thump', *The Observer*, 14 April 1991.

Lezard, Nick, 'Self-publish and be damned', *The Independent*, 8 April 1995.

McGivering, Jill, 'Mo's novel approach to Chinese character', *South China Morning Post* (Hong Kong), 20 April 1991.

Parker, Ian, 'Mo', *Blitz*, July 1987, pp. 32–6.

Pullinger, Kate, 'Creating a hero of our times', *Sunday Times*, 14 April 1991.

Rosser, Nigel, 'Me: Timothy Mo', *South China Morning Post* (Hong Kong), 25 March 1990.

Shannon, David, 'Timothy Mo', *Honey*, November 1983.

Shu Ming, ' "I only want to travel": an interview with Timothy Mo', *Unitas: A Literary Monthly* (Taiwan), vol. 7, no. 12, 1991, pp. 21–5 (in Chinese).

Tonkin, Boyd, 'Postcards from the edge', *The Independent*, 10 July 1999.

Tookey, Christopher, 'In the china-shop', *Books and Bookmen*, May 1986, pp.8–9.

Reviews

(A selected list. Some of the interviews listed earlier also include reviews of the novels.)

THE MONKEY KING

Neve, Michael, 'The Hongkong Beat', *TLS*, 7 July 1978, p.757.

Redmon, Anne, 'A fate worse than death', review of *The Monkey King* and two other titles, *Sunday Times*, 23 July 1978.

Tinniswood, Peter, review of *The Monkey King* and two other titles, *Sunday Times*, 27 July 1978.

SOUR SWEET

Boyd, William, 'Clashes in Chinatown', *Sunday Times,* 25 April 1982.

Evans, Stuart, review of *Sour Sweet*, *The Times*, 22 April 1982.

Lewis, Peter, 'Hongkong London', *TLS*, 7 May 1982, p.502.

Maclean M., 'When man is an island', *Far East Economic Review*, 12 November 1982.

Sage, Lorna, 'Back to Mother Ireland', review of *Sour Sweet* and three other titles, *The Observer*, 25 April 1982.

AN INSULAR POSSESSION

Ackroyd, Peter, 'New voice of our old empire', *The Times*, 8 May 1986.

Ali, Tariq, 'A tale of poppy imperialism', *The Guardian*, 8 May 1986.

Enright, D. J., 'Capturing the China trade', *TLS*, 9 May 1986.

French, Sean, 'Mo's masterpiece: a triumph of ambition', *The Independent*, 2 May 1986.

Kemp, Peter, 'Raging rivalries', *Sunday Times*, 11 May 1986.

Lee, Hermoine, 'Saga of the opium wars', *The Observer*, 11 May 1986.

Quon, Ann, 'Young Mo's epic effort', *South China Morning Post* (Hong Kong), 4 May 1986.

Sutcliffe, Tom, 'Decent opium dealers', *Literary Review*, May 1986, pp. 19–20.

Wilce, Gillian, 'Slow boat', *New Statesman*, 9 May 1986.

Wilson, Dick, 'On the edge of history', *Far East Economic Review*, 18 September 1986.

Yardley, Jonathan, 'Timothy Mo's Asian studies', review of *The Monkey King* and *An Insular Possession*, *The Washington Post*, 26 April 1987.

THE REDUNDANCY OF COURAGE

Ali, Tariq, review of *The Redundancy of Courage, The Guardian*, 18 April 1991.

Billen, Andrew, review of *The Redundancy of Courage, The Observer*, 21 April 1991.

Blaber, Ron, 'Dialogic on imperialism', *CRNLE (Centre for Research in the New Literature in English) Reviews Journal*, no. 1, 1992, pp. 31–3.

Fletcher, Martin, 'State of siege', *New Statesman and Society*, vol. 4, no. 149, 3 May 1991, p. 36.

Friedland, Jonathan, 'An insular occupation', *Far East Economic Review*, 30 May 1991.

Kemp, Peter, 'Conflicting interests', *Sunday Times*, 21 April 1991.

Lezard, Nicholas, review of *Redundancy, Irish Times*, 25 June 1997.

McGivering, Jill, 'Anti-hero running with hopeless cause', *South China Morning Post* (Hong Kong), 20 April 1991.

Miao, Suzanne, 'Mo's rising star plunges with cowardly decision to go into print', *South China Morning Post* (Hong Kong), 9 June 1991.

Sage, Lorna, 'A hotelier in hell', *TLS*, 19 April 1991.

Sharrad, Paul, review of *The Redundancy of Courage, World Literature Today*, vol. 66, no. 2, 1992, p. 405.

BROWNOUT ON BREADFRUIT BOULEVARD
(including reports on the setting up of Paddleless Press)

Barnacle, Hugo, 'Missing the Mo juste', *Evening Standard*, 10 April 1995.

Battersby, Eileen, 'The redundancy of defiance', *Irish Times*, 19 May 1995.

Bradshaw, Peter, 'Messy tale of a modern Imelda', *The Independent*, 15 April 1995.

de Botton, Alain, review of *Brownout, Sunday Telegraph*, 27 April 1997.

Dunmore, Helen, 'Up Corruption Creek', *Observer*, 9 April 1995.

Escoda, Isabel Taylor, 'Who is Timothy Mo?' *Sunday Inquirer Magazine* (Philippines), 18 February 1996.

Fischer, Tibor, 'The unsavoury in full pursuit of the indecent', *The Times*, 20 April 1995

Goring, Rosemary, 'Master loses direction up that creek without a paddle', *The Scotsman*, 23 April 1995.

Harris, Gillian, 'Publishing and damned', *The Scotsman*, 22 March 1995.

Herbert, Susannah, 'Why books are so full of mistakes', *Sunday Telegraph*, 28 May 1995.

Kemp, Peter, 'Darkness visible', *Sunday Times*, 16 April 1995.

Marriott, Edward, 'The sour smell of life in the writers' gutter', *Evening Standard* (London), 21 March 1995.

Mullin, John, 'Timothy Mo set up shop as his own publisher', *The Guardian*, 25 February 1995.

Profumo, David, 'Overpopulation Kills', *The Daily Telegraph*, 8 April 1995.

Taylor, D. J., 'What a carve-up', *The Independent*, 19 April 1997.

Tonkin, Boyd, review of *Brownout* and John Le Carre's *Our Game*, *New Statesman and Society*, 12 May 1995, p. 41.

Yuson, Alfred, 'That brownout Novel (I)', *Philippine Daily Inquirer* (Philippines), 9 July 1995.

——, 'That "Brownout" [sic] Novel (II)', *Philippine Daily Inquirer* (Philippines), 16 July 1995.

RENEGADE OR HALO²

Anon., 'Half a Mo', *Private Eye*, 3 September 1999.

Korn, Eric, 'A practical education', *TLS*, 30 July 1999.

Lezard, Nicholas, 'Too clever for this world', *The Guardian*, 10 July 1999.

Criticism

ARTICLES ON TIMOTHY MO AND HIS NOVELS

'Timothy Mo', in *Contemporary Authors*, vol. 117, Detroit and New York, Gale Research Co., 1986, pp. 301–2.

'Timothy Mo', in *Major Twentieth Century Writers: A Selection of Sketches from* Contemporary Authors', vol. 3,Bryan Ryan (ed.), Detroit and New York, Gale Research Co., 1991, pp. 2081–2.

'Timothy Mo', in *Contemporary Literary Criticism*, Detroit and New York, Gale Research Co., 1988, pp. 257–62.

Hall, Laura, 'New nations, new selves: the novels of Timothy Mo and Kazuo Ishiguro', in A. Robert Lee (ed.), *Other Britain, Other British: Contemporary Multicultural Fiction*, London, Pluto Press, 1995, pp. 90–110.

Ho, Elaine Yee Lin, 'How not to write history: Timothy Mo's *An Insular Possession*', ARIEL: *A Review of International English Literature*, vol. 25, no. 3, 1994, pp. 51–65.

—, 'Of laundries and restaurants: fictions of ethnic space', *Wasafiri*, vol. 21, 1995, pp. 16–19.

—, 'Satire and the national body: Timothy Mo's *The Redundancy of Courage*', SPAN: Journal of the South Pacific Association of Commonwealth Literature and Language Studies, vol. 42–3, 1996, pp. 76–85.

King, Bruce, 'The new internationalism: Shiva Naipaul, Salman Rushdie, Buchi Emecheta, Timothy Mo and Kazuo Ishiguro', in *The British and Irish Novel since 1960*, James Acheson(ed.), London, Macmillan, 1991, pp. 192–211.

Lim, Shirley Geok-lin, 'Who do we name when we say "diaspora"?: race, national identity, and the subject of the subject in Timothy Mo's novels', in *Writing S.E. Asia in English: Against the Grain*, London, Skoob Books, 1994, pp. 91–104.

McLeod, John, 'On the chase for Gideon Nye: history and representation in Timothy Mo's *An Insular Possession*', *Journal of Commonwealth Literature*, vol. 34, no. 2, 1999, pp. 61–73.

Ramraj, Victor J., 'Timothy Mo', *International Literature in English: Essays on the Major Writers*, Robert L. Ross (ed.), New York, Garland, 1991, pp. 475–85.

Rothfork, John, 'Confucianism in Timothy Mo's *The Monkey King*', in *World Literature Written in English*, vol. 29, no. 2, 1989, pp. 50–61.

—, 'Confucianism in Timothy Mo's *Sour Sweet*', in *The Journal of Commonwealth Literature*, vol. 24, no. 1, 1989, pp. 48–64.

Wijesinha, Rajiva, 'Timothy Mo's *The Redundancy of Courage*: An outsider's view of Identity', in *The Journal of Commonwealth Literature*, vol. 28, no. 1, 1993, pp. 28–33.

GENERAL

Achebe, Chinua, *Morning Yet on Creation Day*, London, Heinemann, 1975.

Ahmad, Aijaz, *In Theory: Classes, Nations, Literatures*, London, Verso, 1992.

Anderson, Benedict, *Imagined Communities: Reflections on the Origin and Spread of Nationalism*, London and New York, Verso, 1983.

Ashcroft, Bill, et al. (eds), *The Empire Writes Back*, New York and London, Routledge, 1989.

Barker, Francis, Peter Hulme and Margaret Iversen (eds), *Colonial Discourse, Post-colonial Theory*, Manchester, Manchester University Press, 1994.

Bhabha, Homi K. (ed.), *Nation and Narration*, London and New York, Routledge, 1990.

Boehmer, Elleke, *Colonial and Post-colonial Literature: Migrant Metaphors*, Oxford, Oxford University Press, 1995.

Booth, Wayne, *The Rhetoric of Fiction*, 1961, rpt. Chicago, University of Chicago Press, 1983.

Chatterjee, Partha, *The Nation and its Fragments: Colonial and Post-colonial Histories*, Princeton, Princeton University Press, 1993.

Clifford, James, *The Predicament of Culture*, Cambridge, Massachusetts, Harvard University Press, 1988.

—, *Routes: Travel and Translation in the Late Twentieth Century*, Cambridge, Massachusetts, Harvard University Press, 1997.

Coates, Austin, *City of Broken Promises*, 1967, rpt. Oxford, Oxford University Press, 1987.

Fenton, James, *The Snap Revolution*, New York, Granta, 1986.

—, *Out of Danger*, London, Penguin, 1993.

Frye, Northrop, *Anatomy of Criticism: Four Essays*, 1957, rpt. Princeton, New Jersey, Princeton University Press, 1971.

Geertz, Clifford, 'The integrative revolution: primordial sentiments and civil politics in the New States', *Old Societies and New States: The Quest for Modernity in Asia and Africa*, Clifford Geertz (ed.), New York, Free Press, 1963, pp. 107–13.

Ghosh, Amitav, 'The diaspora in Indian culture', *Public Culture*, vol. 1, no. 1, 1989, pp. 73–8.

Griffin, Dustin, *Satire: A Critical Reintroduction*, Lexington, Kentucky, University of Kentucky Press, 1994.

Hall, Stuart, David Held, Tony McGrew (eds), *Modernity and its Futures*, London, Polity Press and the Open University Press, 1992.

Hall, Stuart and Paul du Gay (eds), *Questions of Cultural Identity*, London, Sage, 1996.

Hamilton-Paterson, James, *Ghosts of Manila*, London, Jonathan Cape, 1994.

Harvey, David, *The Condition of Postmodernity*, Oxford, Blackwell, 1990.

—, *Justice, Nature and the Geography of Difference*, Oxford, Blackwell, 1996.

Highet, Gilbert, *The Anatomy of Satire*, Princeton, New Jersey, Princeton University Press, 1962.

Hutcheon, Linda, *A Poetics of Postmodernism: History, Theory, Fiction*, New York and London, Routledge, 1988.

Hutchinson, John D. and Anthony D. Smith (eds), *Nationalism*, Oxford, Oxford University Press, 1994.

Iyer, Pico, 'The empire writes back', *Time*, 8 February 1993, pp. 48–53.

King, Bruce (ed.), *New National and Post-Colonial Literatures: An Introduction*, Oxford, Clarendon Press, 1996.

King, Paul, *In the Chinese Customs Service: A Personal Record of Forty-Seven Years*, London, T. Fisher Unwin Ltd, 1924.

Kingston, Maxine Hong, *The Woman Warrior: Memoirs of a Girlhood Among Ghosts*, New York, Alfred A. Knopf, 1976.

—, *Tripmaster Monkey*, New York, Alfred A. Knopf, 1989.

Loomba, Ania, 'Overworlding the "Third World"', *Oxford Literary Review*, vol. 13, nos 1–2, 1991, pp. 164–89.

McNeill, William H., *Ethnicity and National Unity in World History*, Toronto, University of Toronto Press, 1986.

Montrose, Louis A., 'Professing the Renaissance: The poetics and politics of culture', in H. Aram Veeser (ed.), *The New Historicism*, New York and London, Routledge, 1989.

Orwell, George, *The Complete Works of George Orwell*, vol. 12, Peter Davison (ed.), London, Secker and Warburg, 1998.

Parker, Andrew et al. (eds), *Nationalisms and Sexualities*, New York and London, Routledge, 1992.

Parker, David, *Through Different Eyes: The Cultural Identities of Young Chinese People in Britain*, Aldershot, Avebury, 1995.

—, 'Emerging British Chinese identities: issues and problems' in Elizabeth Sinn (ed.), *The Last Half Century of Chinese Overseas*, Hong Kong, Hong Kong University Press, 1998, pp. 91–114.

Porter, Jonathan, *Macau: The Imaginary City: Culture and Society, 1557 to the Present*, Boulder, Colorado, Westview Press, 1996.

Pratt, Mary Louise, *Imperial Eyes: Travel Writing and Trans-culturation*, London and New York, Routledge, 1992.

Rawson, Claude, *Satire and Sentiment 1660–1830*, Cambridge, Cambridge University Press, 1993.

Roper, Michael and John Tosh (eds), *Manful Assertions: Masculinities in Britain since 1800*, London and New York, Routledge, 1991.

Rushdie, Salman, *Imaginary Homelands: Essays and Criticism 1981–1991*, London, Granta and Penguin, 1991.

Rutherford, Jonathan (ed.), *Identity: Community, Culture, Difference*, London, Lawrence & Wishart, 1990.

Said, Edward, *Orientalism*, New York, Pantheon, 1978.

—, 'Representing the colonized: anthropology's interlocutors', *Critical Inquiry*, vol. 15, Winter, 1989, pp. 205–25.

—, *Culture and Imperialism*, London, Chatto & Windus, 1993.

Sinn, Elizabeth (ed.), *The Last Half Century of Chinese Overseas*, Hong Kong, Hong Kong University Press, 1988.

Spence, Jonathan D., *The Chan's Great Continent: China in Western Minds*, New York, W. W. Norton, 1998.

Spurr, David, *The Rhetoric of Empire: Colonial Discourse in Journalism, Travel Writing, and Imperial Administration*, Durham, Duke University Press, 1993.

Taylor, Charles, 'The politics of recognition', in Amy Gutman (ed.), *Multiculturalism: Examining the Politics of Recognition*, Princeton, New Jersey, Princeton University Press, 1994, pp. 25–74.

Trilling, Lionel, *Sincerity and Authenticity*, New York, Norton, 1969.

Ventura, Reynald B., *Underground in Japan*, edited and introduced by James Fenton with an Afterword by Ian Buruma, London, Jonathan Cape, 1992.

Waley, Arthur, *Monkey*, London, Allen & Unwin, 1942.

Watson, James (ed.), *Between Two Cultures: Migrants and Minorities in Britain*, Oxford, Blackwell, 1977.

White, Hayden, *Tropics of Discourse: Essays in Cultural Criticism*, Baltimore, Maryland, Johns Hopkins University Press, 1978.

—, 'Historical Pluralism', *Critical Inquiry*, vol. 12, no. 3, 1986, pp. 480–93.

White, Jonathan (ed.), *Recasting the World: Writing after Colonialism*, Baltimore, Maryland, Johns Hopkins University Press, 1993.

Williams, Raymond, *The Long Revolution*, New York, Columbia University Press, 1961.

Young, Robert J. C., *Colonial Desire: Hybridity in Theory, Culture and Race*. London and New York, Routledge, 1995.

Yu, Anthony (transl. and ed.), *The Journey to the West*, 4 vols, Chicago, University of Chicago Press, 1977–1983.

Index

Achebe, Chinua 25, 145
    Anthills of the Savannah 24
    No Longer at Ease 24
    Things Fall Apart 23, 36
Ackroyd, Peter 70
Ali, Tariq 105
Anderson, Benedict 91
    Imagined Communities 89

Ballantyne, R. M. 20
Belo, Bishop Carlos Ximenes 88
Bhabha, Homi 91, 99
Blaber, Ron 105
Book of Five Rings 10
Boxing News 1, 8
Boyd, William 12, 26
*Brownout on Breadfruit
    Boulevard* 1, 6, 7, 16, 19,
    21–2, 27, 94, 109–26, 127,
    147
Buchan, John 21

Charteris, Leslie 21
Conrad, Joseph
    Almayer's Folly 70
    Lord Jim 93

Defoe, Daniel
    Moll Flanders 134
Dickens, Charles
    Hard Times 119
    Our Mutual Friend 70

Eliot, George
    Mill on the Floss, The 70
Eliot, T. S. 22
    Four Quartets 22
    'Journey of the Magi, The'
        24
Elliot, Captain 83

Fenton, James
    Out of Danger 147
    Snap Revolution, The 147
Fielding, Henry 134
    Tom Jones 31, 133, 134
'Fighting their Writing' 8, 9, 13,
    17, 21, 22
Forster, E. M.
    Passage to India, A 119
Frye, Northrop 32
    Anatomy of Criticism 31

Greene, Graham 20, 22

Haggard, H. Rider 21
Hall, Stuart 4, 51
Hamilton-Paterson, James
    Ghosts of Manila 147
Hazlitt, William 20
Hemingway, Ernest 20
Henty, G. A. 21
Hope, Anthony 21
Hutcheon, Linda 74

Insular Possession, An 1, 5, 6, 7,
        15, 17, 19, 22, 28, 43, 69–
        87, 90, 94, 102, 106–7, 141
Isherwood, Christopher
        Journey to a War 85
Ishiguro, Kazuo
        *Artist of the Floating World,
        An* 142
        Pale View of Hills, A 2

Johns, Captain W.E. 21
Jones, James 20
Journey to the West, The (Hsi-
        yu Chi) 10, 31, 32
Joyce, James
        Ulysses 93

Keshen 83
King, Bruce 4, 147
Kingston, Maxine Hong
        Woman Warrior, The 146–7
Kipling, Rudyard 22, 23

Lewis, Peter 12
Lin, Commissioner 83

Masefield, John 20
McEwan, Ian 67
Monkey King, The 1, 5–6, 10, 12,
        13, 17, 22–3, 29–49, 51–3,
        62, 69, 89, 94

Naipaul, V. S. 2, 14, 26, 27
Newell, Mike 67, 68

'One of Billy's Boys' 17, 20
Orwell, George 11

Ramos-Horta, José 88
Ramraj, Victor 147
Rawson, Claude 7, 13
Redundancy of Courage, The 1,
        5, 7, 16, 22, 69, 88-108,
        112, 120-1, 122, 127-8,
        135, 142
Renan, Ernest 95
Renegade or Halo² 1, 6, 7, 16,
        19–20, 21, 22, 109, 114,
        127–43, 148
Rushdie, Salman 2, 14, 23, 24–5,
        26, 144–5, 146
        Midnight's Children 82
        Satanic Verses, The 111

Said, Edward W.
        Culture and Imperialism 23
        Orientalism 23
Sealy, I. Allan
        Trotter-Nama, The 148
Selvon, Sam 2, 67
Shaw, George Bernard 20
Shelley, Mary
        Frankenstein 135, 136–7
Sour Sweet 1, 2, 5, 6, 12–14, 19,
        22, 35, 49, 50–68, 69, 71,
        73, 75, 89, 90, 146–8
Soursweet (film) 67-8
Stevenson, Robert Louis 20, 22

Thackeray, William 20, 134
        Vanity Fair 69, 81, 82, 133
Tingle, Mr 8, 9, 10, 17
Tölölian, Khachig 53
Tolstoy, Leo
        War and Peace 69, 81

Waugh, Evelyn
        Black Mischief 120
        Scoop 119
Westerman, Percy F. 21
White, Hayden 74
Williams, Raymond 35

Yeats, W. B.
        'Second Coming, The' 23